Unleash Quality

Unleash Quality

Build a Winning Strategy for a Culture of Quality That Will Unleash Your Growth and Profit Potential

Arron S. Angle

ASQ Quality Press
Milwaukee, Wisconsin

American Society for Quality, Quality Press, Milwaukee, WI 53203
© 2019 by ASQ.
All rights reserved. Published 2019.
Printed in the United States of America.

26   25   24   23   22   GP   5   4   3   2

Library of Congress Cataloging-in-Publication Data

Names: Angle, Arron S., author.
Title: Unleash quality: build a winning strategy for a culture of quality
  that will unleash your growth and profit potential / Arron S. Angle.
Description: Milwaukee, Wisconsin: ASQ Quality Press, 2019. | Includes
  bibliographical references.
Identifiers: LCCN 2018061269 | ISBN 9780873899833 (pbk.)
Subjects: LCSH: Total quality management. | Quality control--Management.
Classification: LCC HD62.15 .A54 2019 | DDC 658.4/013 —dc23
LC record available at https://lccn.loc.gov/2018061269

ASQ advances individual, organizational, and community excellence worldwide
through learning, quality improvement, and knowledge exchange.

Bookstores, wholesalers, schools, libraries, and organizations: Quality Press
books are available at quantity discounts with bulk purchases for business,
trade, or educational uses. For more information, please contact Quality Press at
800-248-1946 or books@asq.org.

To place orders or to browse the full selection of Quality Press titles, visit our
website at: www.asq.org/quality-press.

Quality Press
600 N. Plankinton Ave.
Milwaukee, WI 53203-2914
Email: books@asq.org

ASQ   Excellence Through Quality™

Contents

List of Figures and Tables

Preface

Was it the title that caused you to pick up this book? Perhaps just plain curiosity regarding the claim of improved profits from something as common as Quality? Most folks would argue that Quality has not been restrained. It's been around for years, so why would it need to be unleashed?

In this book I intend to show how Quality has been restrained by failing to groom and evolve managers outside of the Quality organization to become leaders who understand and embrace a culture of Quality. Likewise, many Quality professionals get caught up in the Lean Six Sigma line of thinking. To wit, they tend to focus more on tool use than on evangelizing a holistic approach to Quality as a behavior applicable from top to bottom within a company. To this point, Quality professionals and managers may not have the tools to recognize nor have the support to drive a cultural transformation across departmental boundaries. If any of this sounds familiar, then please read this book to gain an understanding of how to implement a cultural transformation that will drive long-term sustainable growth and improvement to your bottom-line financials.

You are probably thinking, "But we have Quality programs and what you are suggesting seems 'old school.'" I have been asked this question a number of times. My response has always been, "What and where are you measuring?" Are you measuring manufacturing and service? (Likely yes.) Are you measuring accounting or marketing? (Likely no.) If yes, are these measures driving change or just reporting status? Are these measures aligned with the financial objectives of the company? Are the objectives of the company set out in a strategy that identifies requirements tied to long-term growth and profit? Are these objectives cascaded down into every department in the organization so that every department is required to identify and measure its performance contribution to those aligned strategic objectives?

This really is not "old school" Quality, this is where most companies miss the connection to what a culture of Quality can do for them.

There is power in Quality, but it comes from actions that stem from behaviors. It is the behaviors that have been restrained. Actions around Quality for years have been focused in segments of a company's population, not the entire company. When I speak of behaviors, I am using the word in a holistic sense that applies to every department in a company's structure and organization. In other words, to its culture.

All companies have some form of culture. But how many have you heard brag about a culture of Quality? Years ago, Ford Motor Company bragged about Quality as "Job #1." Looking into the company and its general behaviors, we can see that the statement was more about product rather than about people and their behaviors in all parts of the company. A nice bit of marketing, but it did not represent the culture of the company nor the holistic behaviors of its people, and thus it did not last. This is where most companies fail in their deployment of Quality, by not treating it as a cultural imperative. I hope to provide some guidance on how to correct that in this book.

The flow of this book starts with understanding how a focus on Quality can bring long-term sustainable results to your company's bottom line. You can do this by learning the aspects of a Behavior Based Quality (BBQ) culture and by learning how to unleash an organization's potential by adopting and promoting the behaviors and actions associated with *compliance, prevention,* and *improvement* throughout a company's organization. At this point, the real sustainable profit generation begins.

As the book progresses, we move into the "how" side of things with recommendations on strategy development, consideration to organizational structure, building metrics by department that drive change, and finally maintenance of a BBQ culture.

There are many pieces to the puzzle of establishing a culture of BBQ and there is a lot of ground to cover. The effort is broad in nature and requires deep dives at times, but generally at a high enough level to keep this book an interesting and easy read. Most important, I hope reading this will cause you to think about ways to unleash Quality in your organization.

One last word about culture and behaviors. Please keep in mind that culture is made up of many behaviors. In this book I am proposing compliance, prevention, and improvement (CPI) as the primary tenets of a culture of BBQ. There are many underlying behaviors for each of these three tenets. It is the summarization of many behaviors supporting CPI that brings about a sustainable culture of BBQ, which I will refer to often in this book as BBQ. With that, let's get the BBQ working.

Is this book for you?

I make a lot of statements in this book about the roles and responsibilities of the organization's top-level decision makers, the executives and owners by most people's vocabulary. I could call this an executive handbook on how to build a winning strategy for a culture of Quality. While true, that title doesn't indicate the full intent of this book. Executives may not be familiar with the power of Quality, and so this book is intended to build a foundation of knowledge and familiarity as well as to present a "how to" approach for unleashing Quality to achieve long-term, sustainable bottom-line results to your company's financial statements. For the Quality professional who is already familiar with much of the content: I suggest reading and using this as instructional material for your staff and other managers as to the power of Quality. For those in management who are not Quality professionals: Reading this book will provide you with a knowledge base that you can use for years. As you grow your career and become the top executive, you will have an opportunity to use the principles in this book to guide your managers and set the pace for a BBQ culture. Bottom line? I believe there is something here for every reader. I hope you enjoy the book!

Introduction

This is not your typical book about Quality. If you think Quality is just for manufacturing or service, think again. This is about survival of the fittest in a highly competitive business world. That world has changed dramatically in the last 25 years, moving from manual labor with little automation to highly automated, digitally controlled processes and now toward a future of autonomous provision of goods and services. Private and small businesses have also gone through an evolution. Software, computing, and the way we manage the flow of goods and services and the interface with customers have changed the way we conduct business. The need for Quality and the power it can bring to any business is more important today than ever.

What likely won't become automated is the presence and influence of management. This is where the future of Quality is at stake. Some companies will understand this and embrace Quality as a cultural necessity. Unfortunately, many companies, large and small, have not come to realize what a culture of Quality can do for them. What about you? Do you recognize that Quality must be embraced by every department in your company? If not, this book will help you learn how to set up, organize, and unleash Quality in our digital world to let it work for you in ways that you may not have thought of.

There, I said it! Most books will guide you through the process of Quality assurance or lead you down the path of Lean Six Sigma for cost reduction focused primarily on manufacturing and service functions. While those are certainly aspects of Quality, they are not the complete picture or set of tools that will uncover the hidden profits that you are missing in other parts of your organization with traditional approaches.

How can Quality bring so much to the table?

For years we have been led to believe that Quality is about *assuring* that Quality functions are in place and *controlling* process output through inspection and cost reduction and improvement initiatives. The purpose was to reduce errors. These traditional approaches have channeled our thinking and actions to focus primarily on manufacturing and service functions. Naturally, we believe that these are the largest opportunity areas for cost avoidance and cost reduction and thus where the largest impact to our profits occur. Not too far off the mark, but what about before all this manufacturing output starts, back in the bid and proposal stages prior to design of the product or service? What about design engineering, product costing, financial control, product/program management, marketing, sales, accounting, and more? More specific, if you are not getting Quality correct from the beginning and maintaining it in all these non-manufacturing areas, you are leaving behind unrealized opportunity cost and profit that will fail to optimize your bottom line financial performance.

Why should I read this book?

This approach sounds like a manufacturing book. What if you run a restaurant chain or have a medical practice? What's in it for you? My answer is that Quality is Quality, no matter what line of work you are in. If you're not in the manufacturing business, then please read this book with the knowledge that *manufacturing* is a very broad term; it essentially means the integration of processes that build upon one another to reach an end result output deliverable. That deliverable could be a tool, service, medical examination, properly cooked meal, or much more. So as you read, consider my use of the word *manufacturing* in the context of delivering the service or product you provide to your clients and customers. Again, that product or service could be selling automobiles, packing and moving a family's belongings from point "A" to point "B," building a skyscraper, or owning and serving meals in a restaurant. Quality is Quality, no matter what your line of business.

Do I have your attention now?

Good, then let's get on to building a basis of understanding of what Quality is and what it is not. From there we can show ways to unlock hidden profits and grow your business. We will discuss everything from strategy and structuring a Quality organization to building behaviors that support the construction of meaningful metrics that drive positive change.

Helpful Hint: Although the flow of chapters attempts to build a foundation from "why" to "how," the content is more important than the flow; please feel free to read in any sequence that fits your specific interest.

And the premise of this book is?

Simply put, we want to help company owners, managers, executives, and employees understand how to bring to life or rekindle the behaviors that drive a culture of Quality through compliance, prevention, and improvement methodologies that are supported by organizational structure, accountability, strategy, defined objectives, data collection and use, and much more. This "trilogy" of behaviors is the key to Behavior Based Quality (BBQ). Belief, support, and implementation of BBQ will drive sustainable bottom line results to your business.

Nice words, but what does that mean? I hope to help you understand and appreciate the value, power, and positive impact that Quality and its associated behaviors can have on any business. For larger companies, the establishment of an organizational structure supporting a BBQ culture can bring about profound positive results to your financial bottom line when practiced and supported from the top executive down to the employee level in each department.

To be clear, this book is not about Quality management systems (QMS), which is the process of implementing or maintaining compliance to international standards that your company has or may need to adopt in order to attract or maintain customers. There is plenty of reading material from the American Society for Quality (ASQ) body of knowledge or the International Organization for Standardization (ISO) and other organizations that define the requirements of QMS. You may have a department in your organization that deals specifically with compliance to QMS. Fine, let that department worry about implementation and compliance in that context.

Compliance is pretty well understood from the perspective of building the processes that meet international standards, but by itself it does not generate the structure or behaviors of a learning organization that is constantly in motion to achieve growth and profitability.

Therefore, this book proposes to educate you about the other behaviors that will allow you to lead and build your company culture to a level that adds *prevention* and *improvement* to *compliance,* the three foundational tenets of your Quality culture. I will be referring to them often in this book as CPI. We will focus on the things that bring about prevention and improvement. To have a culture of Quality you will need commitment to all three principles. The interaction of the trilogy of CPI behaviors to achieve a culture of Quality is shown in Figure 1.

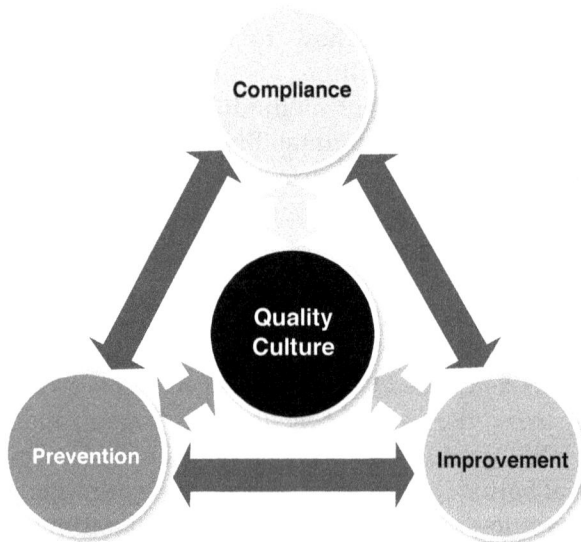

Figure 1   The trilogy of Quality culture behaviors.

Why do Quality issues keep recurring?

Have you ever wondered why Quality keeps coming up as a topic of discussion in senior staff meetings or even in the boardroom? You may be thinking that things just happen. Thus, it would only be natural that the topic comes up where things slip through the cracks and problems occur. But we have a Quality department, you say; why are they not fixing this? Why are they allowing this to happen? Why can't they stop it? We have put fixes in place for past problems of non-conformance; why are the errors recurring?

The answers to these questions come from situations I've observed during my years in various senior management positions and as a consultant to numerous startup and existing companies.

My first observation has to do with the frequency and severity of issues that recur because sustainable solutions were not implemented in the first place. In other words, the rush to fix and move on overshadowed the discovery of an actual solution to the problem. This book will lead you in the process of defining, measuring, and implementing sustainable solutions.

My second observation is that many companies do not adequately understand the power of Quality; they fail to understand the need to assess the existence or health of the culture of Quality in their company. If their solutions to issues are reactionary, driving for a quick fix and then moving on, they likely do not have a culture of sustainable Quality. With this approach, it's likely that the behaviors surrounding Quality practices are not intrinsic to the values they or their employees impart to their daily work activities.

Tough words. But now that I have mentioned *behavior*, please don't think that this book will launch into a long philosophical narrative about the psychology of behavior. As we progress through this book, we will provide a rationale as to how a culture of BBQ culture and the use of Quality tools will bring about sustainable long-term results. A culture of BBQ is one that embraces CPI as the core of Quality behaviors.

A third observation seems more pervasive than it should be. Specifically, there is likely no strategy for Quality. I'm not talking about just within a Quality department; I'm talking about an actual plan to implement, improve, and sustain Quality practices and behaviors throughout a company. This often is an organizational issue having to do with structure, accountability for results, and the placement of the Quality department within the hierarchy of the company in a way that renders it impotent to drive sustainable change to the bottom-line financials. Defining a strategy for Quality is no different from planning for the growth of a company. I would propose that growth requires a Quality product or service, so the obvious question is this. Why wouldn't a company have a strategy for Quality as well? We will address this important aspect in Chapter 4.

Where are you on your Quality journey?

If you are still wondering, the journey is not so much about whether you believe in Quality (who wouldn't), but about whether you support and promote a BBQ culture. So here lies the conundrum. How can you support and promote Quality if you don't know what it is? At one time it was believed that Quality focused on the aspect of "control" as achieved through inspection. Newer thinking, of course, has moved on to Lean Six Sigma methodologies to improve Quality performance. These are outstanding tools that may reduce a product's cycle time by some percentage and may eliminate material cost through redesign or better sourcing, but if the process is still operating with a 10% reject rate, the cost of defects (Quality) has not improved at all. You are just making product faster and cheaper without preventing the causes of the defects. This is not improving Quality.

When you started your Quality journey did you think that Quality only applies to manufacturing processes? Or have you progressed to believing that Quality is a part of every aspect of a company's activity—from finance to sales and marketing and all points in between? Regardless of where you are in your journey, you should ask yourself whether your actions are creating sustainable improvement. If you are not seeing sustainable improved performance from your corrective actions, perhaps you are not measuring the right things. Or perhaps the actions being taken are not addressing the point where poor Quality is actually being generated, the root cause of the issue. It's time to think outside the box. Your first step should be to understand output requirements and determine the right things to measure that identify the total impact of poor Quality. That will allow you to focus your energy in the proper area needing improvement. More on this as we progress through the book.

Why is management singled out?

Because we are setting the introduction to BBQ, let's consider company executives, those senior managers who have profit and loss (P&L) responsibility for a company, division, site, product line, or manufacturing or service function. In other words, it's important to focus on the top decision makers, where the "buck stops"; on the guys or gals in charge of building a business and making money for themselves, their partners, and their shareholders.

In his book *Quality Without Tears,* Philip Crosby argues that Quality without tears is possible. But Quality comes with a lot of pain when it is not managed well or when it is absent from the company culture or from the executives' radar. Clearly there is an order to things and a chain of command for decision making and goal setting. Regardless of what management position you hold, you likely report to higher level of accountability in the company hierarchy. Unless you are at the top (i.e., an owner), you are taking direction from above. Even a CEO usually reports to an owner or a board of directors. Although board members provide guidance and approval for major decisions, they seldom interact with managers or employees or set the pace of the company other than by approving the hire of the CEO who is charged with returning shareholder value. This is not wrong, by the way. By their direction, and by the actions of the CEO and president, the pace of the culture drum is set at the top. That beat, however, is either suppressed or amplified as you get lower into the organization. This is the impact that leadership behaviors have on the culture and momentum of the company.

For those readers not yet at the executive level: Please read on; one day you may be in that position and you will be able to look back at what you learned from this book to set the correct pace for your organization. Let me amplify that last statement: This book is intended to give executives an overview of the broad aspects of Quality beyond the traditional concepts of Quality control and assurance. With this knowledge, you would have a better understanding of the benefits of initiating a culture change to BBQ and be more willing to support your Quality professionals or other managers when they seek such a culture change.

> **Helpful Hint:** *This is one of the reasons for each chapter's preface and takeaway summaries; executives often don't want to spend time reading detail.*

Like an executive brief, this approach provides a summary and an opportunity to dive deeper when there is interest in the subject. Meanwhile the middle manager, directors, and vice presidents from any department who read this book will find detail in each chapter's content that will help them understand more thoroughly the aspects of CPI, organizational matters, meaningful metrics, and much more. They will become future executives, and it is imperative for them to understand the details in order to implement, support, and maintain a culture of BBQ as they grow in their careers.

Is this book just for manufacturing and service readers?

The answer is no. As stated earlier in this chapter, there is something in this book for someone in any line of work or in any position. You may be thinking, I run a restaurant chain or I have a medical practice. Why should I read further? Quality is Quality, no matter what line of work you are in.

> **Helpful Hint:** *As you read, consider my use of the word* manufacturing *in the context of delivering the service or product you provide to your clients and customers.*

Manufacturing is a broad term that essentially means the integration of processes that build upon one another to reach a deliverable output. The deliverable output your business provides could be a tool, service, medical examination, properly cooked meal, or much more. Delivering a properly cooked meal or a medical exam is no less important from a Quality perspective than manufacturing an iPhone or a dishwasher, so please look at the examples or anecdotes provided here to see whether you can relate something to your business.

Takeaway for this chapter: *Few businesses in the world have come to the realization that a Behavior Based Quality (BBQ) culture brings positive results to the company's financial bottom line. We can probably count the big ones on fingers and toes.* Why not more? *I believe it is because we do not walk the talk of management commitment to a BBQ culture. It definitely is not easy. It takes courage, stamina, patience, and belief that sustainable results are only achieved through commitment and support from leaders who commit to Quality as a business imperative. I hope to guide you along the path of success as you read further in this book.*

1

Why Quality?

*Are you kidding? Asking "why Quality?" is like asking if you
drink water. Who is going to say it's a bunch of malarkey?
Of course, we know what Quality is from a product or service
perspective, and we will stand up all day long defending it
as strongly as motherhood and apple pie. The real question
is whether we actually understand how powerful a culture
of Quality can be to any business.*

The real challenge here is whether employees or members of
management can articulate why Quality matters. Most would
say that poor Quality costs the company money and that is
harmful to profit and ultimately to employment. Although very true,
this is only part of the reason why Quality matters.

The next set of institutional answers that one would hear as to why
Quality matters is that Quality control and Quality assurance keep the
company on the straight and narrow of cost control and compliance
to industry standards. Again, this is only part of the reason why
Quality matters.

When thinking of the cost of poor Quality (a metric often referred
to as COPQ), the word "prevention" does not often come into the
conversation. In fact, it's essential to think of prevention in the context
of implementing true solutions to causes rather than simply alleviating
symptoms. In this context, *improvement* is often thought of as taking
waste out of a process while ignoring the reduction of defects. In
a Behavior Based Quality (BBQ) environment, improvement is

thought of as waste reduction through prevention of defects and the enhancement of process efficiencies.

If you are interested in assessing the level of understanding of Quality awareness in your company, look at the Workbook Checklist survey of questions in Appendix B of this book. You can use these to query fellow employees and managers. Although there are really no wrong answers to these questions, I believe the results will provide some insight into how people think about Quality in your company and offer you a way to assess the level of Quality awareness that exists. Most important, the results should give you an idea of whether Quality is part of your company culture. Do people think and behave during their work day as though Quality matters? Do they take accountability for the Quality of their work? Do they feel free to stop any process that is not exhibiting sound Quality behaviors? Or are they more focused on on-time delivery and revenue or profit objectives?

For those of you in management, let's back up a step and ask whether *your* employees recognize that *your* actions support the words in the company's Quality policy, assuming that your company has one.

We will start with a basic premise that no one comes to work to do a bad job. Seems simple enough, right? People typically want to do a good job and are limited only by management support, time, schedule, training, and working environment to perform their jobs at a level that meets management expectations. For clarification, I use "working environment" to describe company culture and the process attributes that are controllable and contribute to being able to effectively perform and achieve a successful process output. Examples would include workplace heating and cooling, training, workstation layout, tools, lighting, operating instructions, and HSE provisions.

When you dive into the details of the previous questions with people who are actually doing the work (as opposed to their supervisors and managers), you may find that lower-level supervisors and managers are not willing to elevate issues or take corrective action due to potential reaction to cost or schedule impacts. Being aware of this may bring you and your management team to a new perception of the reality of Quality. Too often we kid ourselves into thinking that everything is okay because our subordinates said so. Where is the proof? Do you believe the responses? Are there reliable, relevant metrics that provide the proof you need?

Have you had enough of these questions and are you becoming uncomfortable with your doubts? Doubts can generate an environment for learning, so let's move on and give you some history to set the foundation for the discussions to follow. First, the concept of Quality has been around for centuries. Think of the ancient artisans and craftsmen. Stradivarius, for example, was recognized for the Quality of his violins. In more recent times, three modern gurus of Quality rose to prominence during our post World War II industrial revolution: Duran, Deming, and Crosby. I feel compelled to pay homage to these three (in Appendix A). If we do not or cannot learn from our past, we will be destined to repeat it. These three set the foundation for the evolution of Quality as we know it today.

Juran and Deming encountered great challenges while attempting to bring their concepts of Quality to the American industrial machine but found willing listeners in Japan after World War II. Their emphasis on the importance of management engagement and sponsorship of Quality, coupled with the introduction of statistical process control as a Quality tool, turned Japanese manufacturing around and helped it become a global force to be reckoned with in automotive and electronics industries by the late nineteen sixties. These lessons came late to the United States and Europe, where recognition of Quality as a market differentiator didn't start taking hold until the early eighties when Crosby's new concepts of prevention and zero defects started gaining favor.

Although there are many lessons to learn from these three gurus of Quality, please consider that the answer to "why Quality?" does not lie with just one of them. Each has made a contribution to today's Quality philosophy. To Juran, the concept of Quality extends outside the walls of manufacturing; management resistance to change perpetuates the cost of poor Quality. As a systems thinker, Deming believed that a company was a series of interacting systems (management) needing to work in harmony to achieve an output that fell within an acceptable range of variation (Quality). That variation was measured using his statistical process control tools. Crosby felt that the only acceptable performance standard was zero, and that although variation occurred, the goal was to drive variation to zero through prevention measures supported and cascaded down through the organization from top executives. Consider that the common thread of "why Quality?" is that they all believed that Quality improvement was necessary for business survival. More important, they believed it must always be supported and driven by management from the top down as an integral part of the company's culture and an intrinsic part of its DNA, in that Quality behaviors are demonstrated unconsciously, much like breathing.

The challenge with the application of this thinking is that most of those who rise to the highest levels to run companies generally are from engineering, sales, or finance backgrounds. Thus, they often have a perspective of Quality as Quality control (inspection) rather than Quality assurance. Even those who think in more current terms of Quality as assurance may still have not taken the next step to understand and support a BBQ culture in their company through *compliance, prevention,* and *improvement* (CPI). CPI is the necessary approach to achieve total organizational engagement in Quality assurance. Lacking this cultural awareness often results in an executive leading from a "we need to do something about..." approach rather than cascading objectives and cultural behavior requirements down into the organization through assigned actions that are measured.

Takeaway for this chapter: *A sustainable Quality culture is sponsored, supported, and driven by management from the top down into the organization by making all managers and employees, regardless of function, accountable for the Quality performance and sustainability within their sphere of influence and organizational structure. Quality is part of a successful company's DNA. Please read on; there is more in what follows that will take it from theory to practical application.*

2

What is Quality?

In the Introduction, I mentioned that the function of Quality is CPI – compliance, prevention, and improvement. I think it is important to establish this foundation of understanding before we move on to getting your company on the path of sound Quality behaviors and structures.

There are many definitions of the word *culture*. The one that I like and think applies to this book's subject matter is this: "the integrated pattern of human knowledge, belief, and *behavior* that depends upon the capacity for learning and transmitting knowledge to succeeding generations or groups of people." Note that I have emphasized the word *behavior*. Thinking of Quality as a behavior may be new to you. Culture is made up of many behaviors. A culture of Quality is no different. This book establishes compliance, prevention, and improvement as the three tenets of Quality behaviors. To be sure, there are numerous behavior sets under each of these three tenets. Let's discuss each of these elements of Quality separately so that you gain an understanding of what they are and how their integration is the foundation for defining Quality as a behavior.

Compliance: This is likely to be the largest part of your Quality organization. It's easy to be trapped into single-minded "old world" thinking of the Quality function as *control*. I hope to prove in this book that compliance is a far better word than *control*. Like many words, *compliance* carries more than one meaning. Webster's dictionary defines *compliance* as:

"1) The act or process of complying to a desire, demand, proposal, or regimen or to coercion; 2) a disposition to yield to others; 3) the ability of an object to yield elastically when a force is applied: flexibility."

The definition goes on to define *comply* as:

"To conform, submit, or adapt (as to a regulation or to another's wishes) as required or requested."

Side Note: *The American Society for Quality's Body of Knowledge will give you lots of insights as to how to measure and audit for compliance to standards such as ISO or others.*

Let's stick with first and second definitions that more appropriately support the word *comply*. Certainly, one of the major functions of Quality is to implement, guide, monitor, and assure the compliance of a company's processes and procedures to set policies that meet industry standards. From the standpoint of ISO, this is called the Quality management system or QMS. The QMS is the set of company procedures that define how to perform processes as defined by industry standards as critical to the operation of a company to assure a Quality output. These functions will range from design to financial control, procurement, and all points in between. To this point, compliance is about whether or not employees are following those set procedures. To be clear, this is not about the cost or efficiency of the process; it's about whether the process is being followed in accordance to the documented procedures and whether those procedures meet the intent of the ISO or other certification standards. Important to note is that this is not necessarily about whether the process is generating errors or whether the process is efficient. As I mentioned, there are many books written on how to implement, audit, and maintain a QMS. That is not the area that we will focus on in this book.

In this book we will be focusing on a subtly different compliance: compliance (conformance) to requirements. Compliance to QMS is about "how" things are done. Compliance for our use is about "what." Although compliance and QMS are similar, QMS deals more with the "how" of a process. Thus, even with the latest edition of ISO standards, it's possible to have a compliant design process that may still be generating non-conformances.

Here's an example to make this clearer: QMS requirements for design tell you the *"how"* steps of the design process you will follow regardless of "what" you are designing. Our focus will be on "what" we are designing. To do that, we must first establish the output requirements of each step of the design process. At a high level, this is typically accomplished by writing a specification at the beginning of the design process; this allows the engineers know what the specifics of the customer's needs are in order for the design to meet the output requirements defined by the customer. This sounds simple enough, but if the requirements are not mutually agreed upon, the output can look something like the classic cartoon (Figure 2) from the 1970s.

At a lower level, this means defining the output requirements for each step of the design; not just each part, but each step for each part. It sounds simple, but not establishing the lower-level process step output requirements is where most design errors originate. I have used engineering as the example, but the issue of setting requirements is the same for any functional process step in any department. As

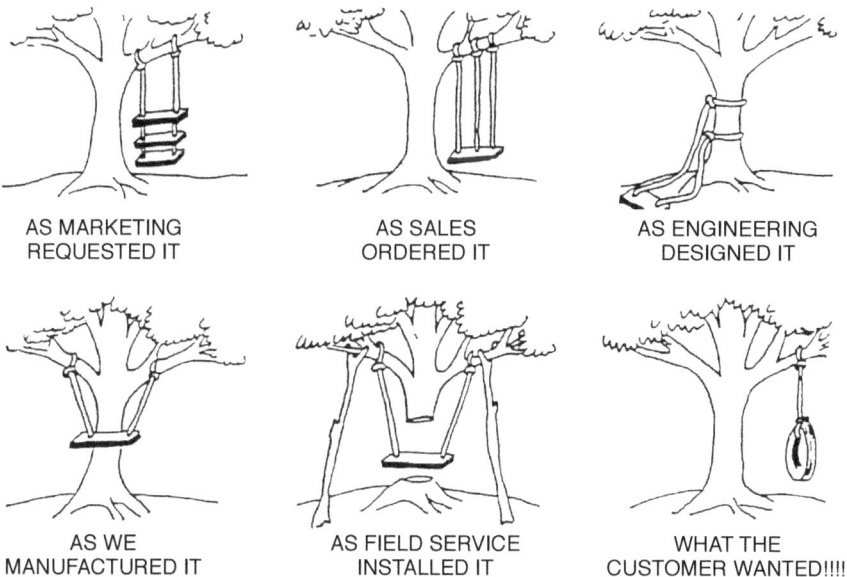

Figure 2   Tree Swing picture from 1970s.   CREDIT: Businessballs.com (Ack T & W Fleet).

simple as setting requirements may sound, think about something as ordinary as ordering pizza. Unless you have no concerns about the outcome and are willing to live with what you get, saying, "I want a pizza" is insufficient. What size? Square pan or round? Thin or original crust? What toppings do you want? And so on. We are presented with options all the time. Often we are given the opportunity for customization even for the most basic of wants. Go into a Starbucks some time and try to order a plain black coffee. Will that be tall, grande, or venti?

What does this mean, you ask? Well, aside from the monitoring side of compliance, a very important function of your Quality organization is to work with all departments to establish what their internal and external customers want as process output. We will discuss more of this next when we consider prevention, but to say the least we must start at the initial stages of product development.

In engineering design, requirements may be established in R&D or by a request for quotation (RFQ) from a customer. This is the first opportunity and the best place to gain full knowledge and awareness of what your customer wants in as much specific detail as possible. If you don't get them correctly identified and mutually agreed upon at this point, months of delays and many dollars will be wasted in your attempt to properly meet your customer's requirements. To summarize, your compliance team needs to assess the Quality requirements of product design in the RFQ stage and throughout the development process for compliance to customer specs and industry standards. For service companies, requirements must be clearly understood and mutually agreed upon at the contractual signing of a service agreement.

The examples used have focused on what we define as a company's product output. While this is very true, the concept of conforming to process output also applies to internal company process deliverables within and between the various functional departments. Importantly, each step in a process requires conformance as well. To summarize, compliance in the context of this book is conformance to the mutual agreement of requirements between customer and supplier.

Prevention: This word shouldn't need much clarification, but let's be sure we are on the same level of understanding. *Prevention* as used in Quality means to keep unspecified things from happening. For example, if we are operating a process in compliance to specifications, prevention is about assuring that any form of noncompliance is prevented from occurring. Let's now take this one step further. If each process step has an output, and if requirements for the output have been established and mutually agreed upon between the process step owner and the next process step owner (customer), then *prevention* means to maintain compliance to those requirements so that non-conformances are not generated as part of the output; they are prevented. At the very least, prevention is about setting our standard at zero non-conformances and perpetually minimizing the occurrence of non-conformances by assessing the causes of failures and putting corrective (prevention) measures in place.

Prevention of non-conformances starts with measurement. Consider that you can't change what you don't measure. If you consistently measure the performance of your process as compliance to requirements and the base causes of non-compliance are also accounted for, then you are gathering the data to which change can be applied. Thus, one of the most important aspects of prevention is measuring the right things. Of course we measure the right things, you say. To this I would respond, great if you do, but are you sure? Establishing the right performance metrics provides one of the greatest opportunities for any company to start on the path to prevention. Here is an example that I came across while managing a software engineering department.

Figure 3, Path 1 illustrates a software development metric defining errors per lines of code as a percentage to target. You can see that performance is a bit erratic but trending toward the target of 98% good code when tested for the first time. One could be lulled into complacency by tracking the trend noted as Path 1; all seems to be heading in the right direction. The Path 2 chart tells a different but supporting story; things appear to be getting better. The "other" issues have been taken to zero and remain there. Spelling errors in lines of code have also been reduced significantly.

However, not much improvement has been made to command line errors and code linkage errors. The problem with both of these charts is that they do not indicate the cost impact of these errors. For example, if the solution to spelling errors takes five minutes of spellcheck to survey 10,000 lines of code, then that is a low cost. On the other hand, if linkage errors require 10 hours of consulting time to debug each error at a cost of $200 per hour, it amounts to a significant impact in dollars and time delay. It's the same with command line errors.

S/W First Pass Yield

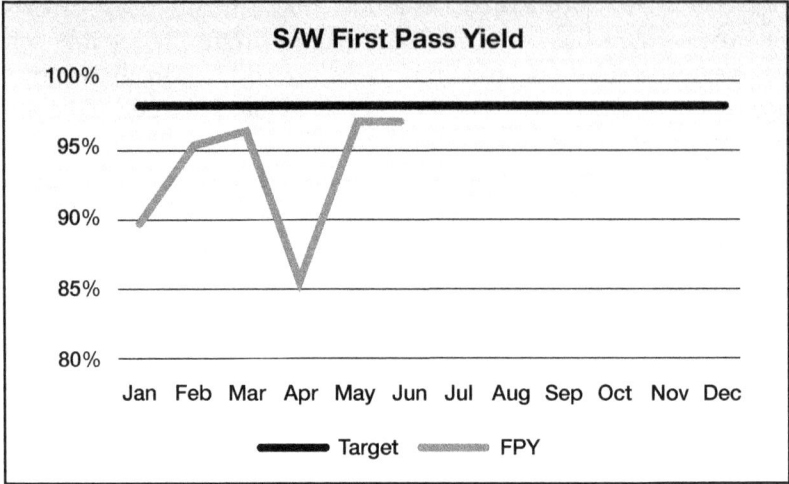

Path 1

S/W Code Defect Causes

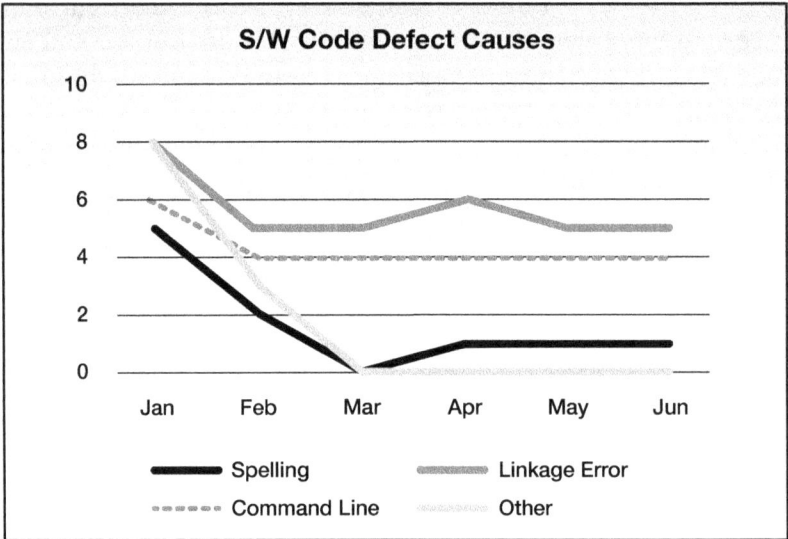

Path 2

Figure 3 Two software development Quality metrics.

These metrics as designed are not identifying the impact of errors in terms of cost and delays. Essentially, they are just pretty pictures that seem to indicate that measurements are being taken and tracked. But to what purpose?

When properly assessed, the delays caused by the errors may affect your market introduction timing as well as bottom-line financial forecasts and/or actuals. The point here is that these metrics are missing an important factor that can drive change. That factor is the monetary impact of errors. The Path 2 metric seems to support that trending toward the target of 98% yield is under control, but there is no evidence of the cost impact. Equally important, why would the target be set at something less than 100%? To drive new thinking, we changed these metrics by assessing and monetizing the impact of each error type and adjusted the target to 100%. Making the cost impact visible allowed heightened awareness of the impact of errors. This made it possible to prioritize solving and preventing the highest-impact errors first and then move on to the next highest-impact errors for corrective and preventive action. For this project, 100% performance was achieved and maintained in just three months.

Figure 4 provides another example that I ran into with a client we will call Bill's Weld and Cladding Shop. They were very proud of the performance of their weld team as shown in the Path 1 chart. Bill's had operated for the last month prior to my arrival with a welding first pass yield (FPY) of 90%. Broken down, this means that 90 welds out a hundred were conforming to requirements and 10 welds were non-conforming or rejects. The shop had met its goal of 90% FPY for that month. Everyone was happy and a celebration was scheduled at the noon break to recognize the efforts of the team. All seems in order, right?

Not wanting to spoil the celebration, I later discussed with them that there were several other paths that could have been taken during the month. One path would have been to "keep on keeping on" with the same effort and only measure conforming versus non-conforming welds, as was the case in Path 1. A second path would have been to measure the causes of the non-conformances as they occurred, measuring the FPY as well as a lower level measurement of the fundamental causes of non-conformances. It's important to remember that if you know the cause of a non-conformance, you can assess whether it is a process anomaly, a trend, or some other failure mechanism. In any case, corrective actions could have been determined in order to (wait for it…) prevent the reoccurrence of the non-conformance.

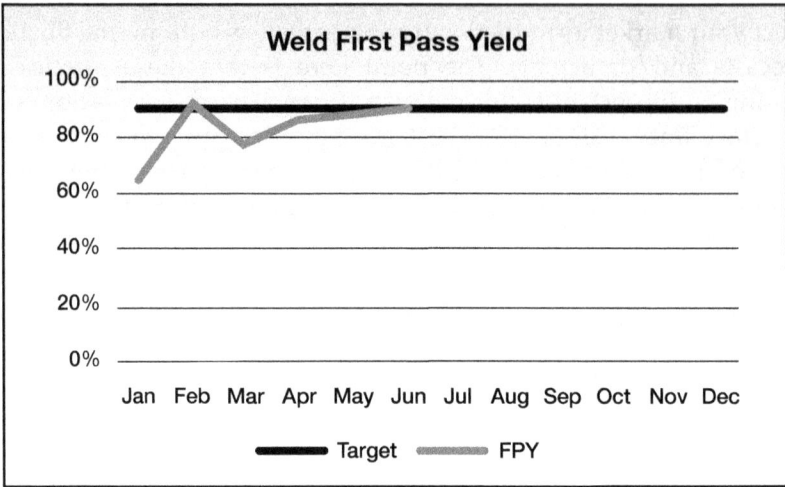

Path 1

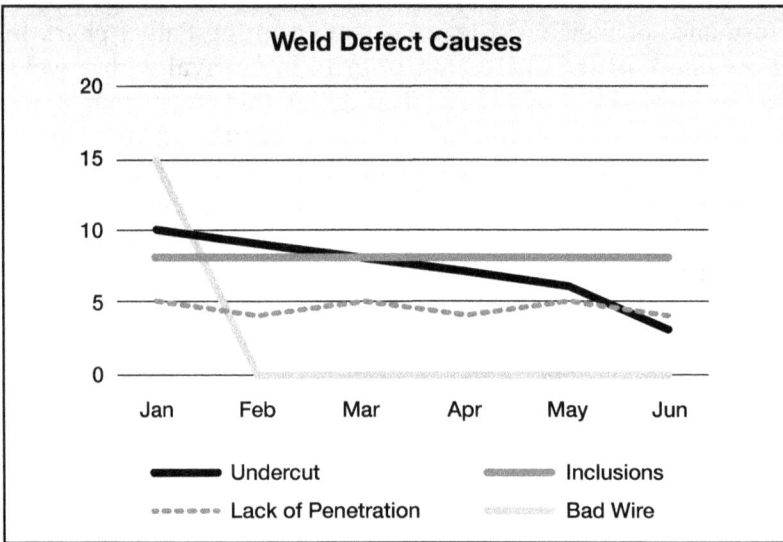

Path 2

Figure 4 Weld performance metrics.

As a reader of this book, I hope you will see the opportunity that is presented when you look a bit deeper into measurements. More important, rather than settling for what the industry may consider good performance, why not strive for "best" performance? Set your standard at zero non-conformances; when you hit 90% FPY, recognize your team for great effort and challenge them to do better. Encourage the use of tools to assess barriers that are hindering improved performance, then implement further corrective action to prevent further errors. In Figure 4, the Path 2 chart gives a visual reading of the causes of defects. From this chart you can see that the defect of "Inclusions" (typically contamination) has not improved over time like the other reject modes. To take welding performance to the next level, start here in order to understand what is creating inclusion issues and then put corrective actions together to prevent further occurrence of this failure mode. Used together, the two charts provide the measurement that brings about recognition and positive change. Now ask yourself which path provides a greater opportunity to exceed the 90% FPY objective that was set. If you are satisfied with the status quo and willing to live with a constant 90% FPY, then the first path is the direction for you. Many companies operate this way without thinking any further. They have limited their capability and profit potential by settling on what they believe is good industry performance.

Here's another thought for the profit thinkers. Path 1 that Bill's Weld and Cladding Shop took accepts that 10 welds out of a hundred will be non-conforming. Typically, companies build this waste into their product costing. This also typically assumes that only one rework takes place to cure the non-conformance. Even worse, most companies do not measure second- or third-pass yields; they have no measurement of the actual number of non-conformances beyond FPY. Assume for a moment that a weld repair for inclusions costs $100 each. Ten non-conformances equals $1,000 that the takers of Path 1 have baked into their product cost either directly or indirectly via overhead amortization. If, for some reason, two non-conformances are generated during the re-weld process, then an additional $200 of cost is incurred by the company. Since this is not in the product costing, the additional cost of second-pass rework directly impacts profit margin. Unfortunately, the source of this added cost is often not recognized and management is left reporting to the board of directors a profit performance issue that is not clearly understood or has been misdiagnosed.

To summarize, *prevention* means taking corrective action on measurable events that vary negatively from set standards of performance or compliance. I want to emphasize, again, that this is not limited to manufacturing or engineering. Non-conforming process variation can occur in finance, HR, or any other department in a company. What is important is to set measurements for each department that capture variation and its causes wherever they exist, then take corrective action to prevent them from recurring. So here is the test: Which path leads to greater profit potential?

Now consider the example of a restaurant where ten percent of the orders cooked were returned to the kitchen for issues related to customer expectation. How long do you think the restaurant would stay in business if it did not address the issues that caused the returned orders?

Improvement: As you might guess, non-conformance is a form of waste. Once we have eliminated non-conformances through prevention, there is still room for improvement. This is where we will work diligently to effect the elimination of other forms of waste. If no effects are being generated, then how can there be other forms of waste? Consider milling a 2-inch piece of metal down to an inch to meet finish requirements. Wouldn't it save material cost if you were able to buy a 1.5-inch piece of metal instead? This is a form of waste. Making this change would save the cost of the extra half inch of material as well as the labor to mill it. This is the *improvement* aspect of Quality behavior. Modern Quality philosophy labels this approach of waste reduction as "Lean" or Lean process improvement. Having a culture of Behavior Based Quality (BBQ) will promote that all employees, regardless of position and organization reported to, are accountable for the Quality of daily work and obligated to say *"stop"* when they observe an action or behavior that is not compliant to procedures, standards, or specifications. This is the same type of behavior that we expect from a safety culture. If your company has a good behavior-based culture of safety, then your team should have an easier time understanding the rationale behind introducing and adopting a BBQ culture. However, don't take this transition too lightly or believe it will be easy. There will be people who are unwilling to make the jump to BBQ culture. These people tend to be stuck in old-world thinking about Quality and don't hold themselves accountable because they believe Quality is someone else's job.

Real improvement is more than the suggestion box that sits vacant, waiting for good ideas to be submitted. It is the active engagement of employees who are continuously looking for better ways to do their job by taking forms of waste out of the processes they perform. Waste in this context can mean excessive time to do the job (labor); excessive consumption of material (material); excessive process throughput (time and/or labor), and so forth. The causes of waste may vary and may not be related to non-conformances. Here's an example: a design calls for a 5-inch piece of metal that will be machined down to 2 inches in diameter, essentially rendering 3 inches of machining as wasted material and wasted machine time. Solution: specify 2½ inch diameter material and finish machine to 2 inch diameter. This renders a substantial material savings that reduces product cost and supports higher profit margins and/or improved competitiveness.

Now let's explore waste that is not impacting compliance but, if left unattended, may result in a continuation of excessive labor and time to perform a function. This is an indirect function that has the opportunity to reduce cost and add to bottom-line profit. A culture of Quality will always be mindful of indirect costs that are typically part of an overhead or general and administrative (G&A) adder to product costing. These areas should be considered rich with opportunities for improvement.

As an example, consider that you have eliminated all errors (non-conformances) in accounts payable transactions that require journal adjustments, refunds, and corrected payments. The improvement allowed the function to now be performed by five people. The process still takes seven days due to complications and interdepartmental analysis and transactions. One of the A/P clerks has come up with a great idea for an improvement that takes a day out of the process but still seems to require five people to perform the A/P function. One of the company's improvement facilitators comes to the department to map the process and work through each process step and its requirements. The requirements of the process are validated by the team, which recognizes that the A/P process can now be performed by just four people. The process is adjusted and put into operation with four people. The team has now saved a day of processing and a day of labor cost. Looking deeper, we can see that one process day saved resulted in five man-days of labor saved; the reduction of five people to four people saved four man-days of labor. The day saved was actually waste from the prior process. To eliminate this waste, the solution is to find other work in the company for the person no longer needed to perform the A/P function. If there are no internal transfer opportunities, it may be necessary to let someone go. That's a worst-case scenario. On the other hand, assume a capable employee who may fit other roles with minor training updates. Imagine the power of using this "excess" person in a new role that was necessitated by growth. This is a great opportunity to show your finance team that their improvement was recognized and that improvement can have a positive outcome. Another artifact of this type of action is that you may be able to keep staffing level, rather than bringing on an additional headcount. Thus, you may get two savings out of this waste elimination.

Side Note: I mentioned "improvement facilitator" above. At one time, General Electric (GE) made an art form of this function by essentially decreeing that all salaried employees earn and maintain a Green Belt certification within six months of their hire date. Moreover, any person who desired to progress within the company was required to earn and maintain a Black Belt certification or higher. I won't go into the description or requirements of these certifications other than to say that like the martial arts, the nomenclature it was patterned after, the color of the belts denoted levels of competency in the art of identifying areas needing improvement through a process of define, measure, analyze, improve, and control (DMAIC), using "Lean" improvement and Six Sigma measuring and assessment tools. A belt of color is not a requirement to be a facilitator, but certainly provides a basis of understanding on how to effectively use the tools of Quality.

Improvements may be tackled individually or by a group led by a facilitator who has an understanding of the tools needed to achieve improvement. As with prevention, improvement begins with measurement. The saying "You can't change what you don't measure" is countered negatively by "You won't measure what you don't want to change." Not wanting to change may sound a bit harsh, but think of the familiar axiom. "Well, that's the way it has always been done and no one has complained, so why change now?" This is one of my personal "hot" buttons. Yours, too? I believe there is no greater threat to improvement than the unwilling mind. Not recognizing why change is necessary is the second greatest threat to improvement. Together, these two poor behaviors will bring down the performance of a department while spreading the disease further into your company and ultimately impacting profitability, competitiveness, and growth. These are negative cultural behaviors. Most employees come to work and want to do a good job. If they develop ways to improve their job function but are not recognized for their efforts or encouraged to do more, they will eventually adopt an attitude. Why should I care if the company doesn't care? This leads to either complacency or to the departure of good, energetic employees from your company for greener pastures. In either case, this is not the culture you want to foster.

As the leader of your company, you will find the greatest success when you foster and promote a Quality culture supporting the behavior of compliance, prevention, and improvement. This trilogy represents the cornerstones of BBQ and will render continuous improvement and sustainable profitability to your bottom-line financials. When the behaviors are like breathing, you don't have to think about it; it just happens.

To summarize, *improvement* is the Quality function of facilitating change in organizations that brings about lower operating costs, faster throughput of processes, and the elimination of unnecessary waste while maintaining a culture and performance standard of zero non-conformances. Although all employees are accountable to contribute to improvement, it is the role of the Quality function to translate, promote, and facilitate the top executive's cultural imperative of continuous Quality improvement in all departments.

Takeaway for this chapter: *The behaviors related to compliance, prevention, and improvement provide the foundation for a Quality culture of continuous process improvement. A successful company must understand and comply with requirements, must use prevention as the basis for eliminating non-conformances, and must continually strive to improve by eliminating waste in all of its unintended forms that add cost to the company, erode profits, and constrain growth. Compliance, prevention, and improvement (CPI) is the cornerstone of a sound Behavior Based Quality (BBQ) culture that will bring sustainable results to your company.*

3

Who Owns Quality?

Are you now at a point of understanding that Quality is one of the primary factors in the success of a company? If you aren't there yet, consider this: although a company may have groundbreaking technology or an incredibly low product price, poor Quality will not bring sustainable repeat business growth or long-term profitability once early adopters have passed judgment on the product or service.

Before we jump into who owns Quality, let's take a leap into the common industry practice of relying on a Quality organization to maintain control of or improve Quality performance, typically at the product or service level. Some would consider this an environment of Quality control versus Quality assurance, so let's tackle these definitions first. Quality control, as the name implies, is about the control of Quality, typically through inspection operations and in some companies also by testing. The American Society for Quality (ASQ) defines Quality control as "the observation techniques and activities used to fulfill requirements for Quality." In other words, inspection. ASQ defines Quality assurance as "the planned and systematic activities implemented in a Quality system so that Quality requirements for a product or service will be fulfilled." In other words, providing the assurance that Quality processes are in place. You can find more information on this at the ASQ website (www.asq.org).

Note that both of these definitions use the word *requirements*. Seems very clear and simple, but it is actually complex. Most often we think of external customer requirements that must be met. In other words, the requirements of the end product. Many end products require a series of potentially complicated process steps. Material purchasing is a good example. It requires delivery, inspection, fabrication, assembly, test, finishing, and final assembly and inspection. Each of these process steps has input and output requirements that must be met prior to hand off to the next process step operator (internal customer) in order to comply with the final customer requirements. If a single requirement along this chain is not met before passing on to the next process operator, it is highly probable that the final product will not comply with requirements.

This is where I hope you begin to understand that Quality can be defined as a series of process steps linked together as part of a system of process steps to achieve end objectives (deliverables). Moreover, this system of process steps must meet customer (internal or external) requirements. Assuring that each process step's requirements are well understood and achievable is where the "assurance" part of Quality is most often ignored. Ignoring individual process step requirements and focusing on the final product or end result opens a wide gap of compliance to individual process step requirements that lead to non-conformances and added product/process costs. In Quality systems, meeting the multiple process step requirements to achieve the end objective's requirements can be one of the most challenging aspects of assuring Quality. We will discuss this in greater detail further on in this book.

Quality got its start as a means to identify and control the *absence* of Quality. Today's "enlightened" approach is to prevent the absence of Quality by measuring the variation in processes and determining and implementing conformance, prevention, and improvement solutions (as defined in the preceding chapter) in all aspects of the work environment. The foundation for solutions is measurement. Perhaps your own company is structured such that a Quality function monitors factory performance, service level performance, and other product-related functions.

Notice that I identified product and service metrics. If you take to heart my message from the last chapter, you will realize that other departments are accountable to measure Quality as well. Commonly, metrics are gathered from departments and reported by the Quality function. Department managers look at the data and perhaps challenge offending performer(s) as to why things are going so poorly. The immediate question is this. Who is doing the challenging, the department manager, the Quality manager, or even company leadership in periodic management reviews? Mildly progressive companies may go so far as to ask about cause and corrective actions and may take action on this information. More progressive companies may even insist on a timeline for the intended corrective action. However, all too frequently there will be little to no management follow-through on this data other than a repeat of the reporting cycle as just described. Management follow-through is one of the strongest messages that you, as a leader, can provide to your employees. It demonstrates your commitment to understanding issues and bringing issues and solutions to the table for discussion. Cascading your commitment to follow-through and insisting on corrective action to your direct reports and further down through your organization demonstrates the company's cultural commitment to Quality behaviors.

Reminder: *In the introduction I mentioned that Quality is not just for manufacturing companies. It is easier to talk in this context, but I want to remind you that the same principles hold true for your family dentist, pizza shop owner, pharmacy, and auto shop. Now back to the topic.*

It is important to understand the attitude of your managers and employees toward your Quality organization. Quality folks are frequently perceived to be the "police." If this is a result of Quality department behaviors, I suggest that there is work to be done to change that perception. Another common perception of Quality professionals is that they are simply driving the collection and maintenance of Quality metrics, assuming that you have them. This is another perception (or behavior) that must be changed. On a more positive note, if Quality professionals are thought of as solution facilitators for your company, it's a step in the right direction. The behaviors of your Quality professionals can have an impact on perceptions of Quality. It is important that inspection be thought of as keeping errors and non-conformances out of the hands of customers. Driving the collection and maintenance of departmental metrics is not the typical role of Quality; each department should be accountable for Quality performance, inclusive of collection and maintenance of metrics. A Quality department is typically well suited to assist with or facilitate solutions to Quality performance issues. Eventually every department (payroll, engineering, sales) realizes it has a stake in Quality, not just the factory or service teams.

You may think that because Quality folks are "numbers people," they are the logical ones to maintain metrics. The simple truth is that this is exactly why Quality folks are often thought of as the company "police" and metrics are not taken seriously because they "belong" to the Quality organization. So, let me be clear. Quality departments can include facilitators to help with pulling together and analyzing metrics, but it should be the responsibility of individual departments to develop and maintain their Quality performance metrics. This is part of the Behavior Based Quality (BBQ) cultural change being proposed in this book. Until metrics are developed and maintained by the department accountable for the measured results, "ownership" will likely never gain the level of traction needed to truly bring about positive sustainable improvement in Quality performance.

Most companies know how to measure manufacturing Quality. Performance statistics are typically provided in process yield percentage or defect rates per million opportunities (DPMO), which translates into a sigma level of performance (e.g., Six Sigma). Process variation and yield percent are other metrics that can be used. These metrics are sometimes reported to management only. In more progressive companies, metrics may also be visible at the work location within the accountable department, where team members and all who walk by can view them.

As an executive leader you should be asking whether your metrics are just "pretty charts on the wall" or whether they are actually being used to identify issues and drive improvement. An easy check would be to walk through your factory or departments with metrics on display and check the revision dates on the charts. If the measurement is weekly and the chart is more than a week old, it's likely they are for show and not for change. An organization focused on improvement will maintain these charts and always keep them current.

We are accustomed to seeing metrics for service or manufacturing. As a leader, ask yourself when was the last time you saw a metric for payroll performance or metrics that measured the actual performance of engineering *during* the design process (i.e., design review findings/corrections), not after (i.e., rejected parts). Did you recognize in this last example that measuring design performance at a design review is actually a form of prevention?

If we accept the thinking that all departments are accountable for measuring the results of their output, why would we put our Quality success in the hands of a single organization such as Quality department to drive improvement? The operative word here is "drive." I would propose that to "facilitate" improvement would be a better choice of words.

Note that it was not specified in this chapter where the Quality function should report organizationally. My intention is to stress the importance of ownership of accountability rather than focus on a reporting structure. I have seen companies where Quality reported to HR, finance, manufacturing, and engineering as well as to top executives such as COO or CEO. To facilitate a cultural change, where do you think Quality fits best? There is no "one size fits all" organizational solution. Many factors such as product line, company size, skills, and more can set an organizational structure. Flexibility as company dynamics change is also key. Ask this question: where will a sustainable culture of BBQ be led from in your company that supports personal accountability for Quality performance and bottom-line results?

Takeaway for this chapter: *Every employee in every function in a company "owns" accountability for Quality performance. Managers are accountable for the Quality performance of their functional area of responsibility. Executives are accountable to insist on Quality by promoting and supporting CPI (compliance, prevention, and improvement) behaviors in all areas of the company. When asking any employee "Who owns Quality?," the answer should be "I do!" They should be able to articulate why.*

4

Do You Have a
Strategy for Quality?

---

*I have to ask: do you have a strategy for Quality? I've asked
this a number of times of clients. After a few blank stares and
questioning looks, I quickly fill the silence. I'm sure you have
a strategy for sales and profit objectives, I say; I'm wondering
whether you have one for Quality. A strategy for Quality ties
directly to growing a company and improving bottom-line
financials.*

After letting them off the hook, I continue with my story that
a top-level strategy typically involves adding value to the
company by increasing sales and growing profits. This usually
causes heads to nod in the affirmative. Of course, the meat of any
strategy has to do with how this strategy will be implemented and
what will be the expected outcomes.

Then I ask whether their strategy includes using Quality to add
value in order to grow profits and sales. The response is often blank
stares, because this is not a typical approach to strategy. Quality
is often thought of simply as a tool to get rid of those pesky non-
conformances. Yes, there is a cost/profit contingent with that thinking.
But does this actually percolate up to the executive level, resulting in a
strategy that uses Quality in every department to eliminate errors and
reduce all forms of waste across the entire organization? The answer
is most often "no." Even when the answer is "yes," often the focus is
solely on manufacturing/service initiatives rather than on a holistic
approach to building a Quality strategy across the entire organization.
Specifically, every department is challenged to define its contribution

to improving Quality that positively impacts the bottom-line financial performance. These contributions then roll up to contribute to the company's overall financial performance. Note that this is not about slashing budgets; it's about improving efficiency and preventing errors. When this type of strategic thinking is implemented, it takes us into the behavioral aspect of Quality, where we use CPI to reinforce Behavior Based Quality (BBQ) to drive sustainable results.

Some people think that a simple business strategy is all that is required: grow bigger faster. Clearly this is not a strategy; it contains no specific objectives or targets. More importantly, it does not establish or promote a cultural imperative regarding how the strategy will be executed. The *how* is what establishes acceptable behaviors for the company to move toward.

Case Study

Years ago, I worked for a defense company where every August we would start a detailed five-year planning process that would distill down to the next year's annual operating plan (AOP). The company believed that if it defined long-term objectives (this was always and only about growing the business), then the natural fall-out of that would be what needed to be done in the next fiscal year to achieve that objective. Large binders of information would be presented to board members to show what sales and marketing would do to capture market share, what monies would be spent, and what capital investments were needed to support the growth.

You might think that this sounded pretty darn comprehensive. The answer is yes, partially. In fact, the AOP was seldom met, and this process is general practice in much of corporate America. You might ask why the AOP was often missed. The answer is twofold: First, the AOP was generally developed as a budgetary process with consideration to gross margin achievement rather than actual requirements to achieve growth results. Thus, critical infrastructure spend was often eliminated. Second, the plan was not backed up by a strategy that defined barriers to be overcome in order to achieve the objective. Thus, the successful achievement of the AOP was random.

The missing piece to the strategy puzzle was actually quite simple: *define the barriers to success and develop plans to overcome them.* That strategy, when deployed, would address and remove the barriers to success, thus giving way to the operating plan. When this critical input was shown to the company by a consulting group focused on strategy deployment, the company started to become successful in achieving its AOP and ultimately achieving its five-year plan.

I carried this great story with me for years as *the* way to build an internal strategy within a company's framework in order to move a company toward success. As I evolved in my Quality thinking, I realized that this strategy, as good as it was, was flawed in its development because it did not include the identification of Quality-related barriers to success. Thus, it was lacking a critical piece of the total strategy that would identify the actions supporting compliance, prevention, and improvement necessary to remove barriers. Removing the barriers with strategic action would allow enhanced contribution to bottom-line total company financial and growth objectives. Quality in this context, of course, means all forms of waste, including non-conformances in every department. Barriers to success can often be defined as Quality related. As an example, see the case study below.

Case Study

In the middle of the tech bubble, I was brought in as an engineering turnaround manager for Telxon Corporation, which designed and built portable computing devices. At that time, the time span between product concept and manufacturing/market introduction was just over 36 months. In this fast-evolving and competitive market, this lengthy development process equated to a going-out-of-business plan and thus a barrier to success, if not improved. Upon study of the design, review, and testing processes, the barriers were determined to be excessive time spent in both electronic and mechanical engineering development. The cause was identified as repetitive design errors resulting from the fact that various subassembly design teams were located in remote locations in the company with little or no communication between them.

Case Study (cont.)

It was also found that many of the assemblies were not manufacturable due to poorly fitting parts or attachment devices located in inaccessible areas of the assembly; these were returned to engineering for redesign. The strategy to remove the barriers to success was rather simple: The design teams were moved into product-centric areas in a single location to promote enhanced communication among electronic, software, and mechanical engineers. Senior manufacturing engineers were brought from a manufacturing plant into the design team in order to participate in the design process, rather than weighing in after design completion. In three short months of activity following this new strategy, the design-to-production throughput was shortened to just under nine months with a flawless introduction to the manufacturing process. The result was a profound financial contribution to the bottom line from the standpoint of cost avoidance and labor savings. Even more important was the ability to beat competitors to market with new products.

The case study seems hard to imagine in today's world of highly automated design and testing processes. Even with automation, getting to that point is a complex endeavor consisting of many process steps and usually thousands of lines of code. Consider the tools available to a software engineer assigned to write code to automate a process today. The tools are extremely capable, but highly complex. The more complex we become in our processes and product development, the greater the need for a strategy based upon the CPI principles of Quality.

I have brought the trilogy of CPI behaviors back into the conversation in order to show that integrating them into the strategy-building process can lead to solutions and actions that improve company performance. This is the essence of a culture that embraces BBQ. As a company evolves to a BBQ culture, Quality thinking becomes part of its fabric or DNA. Thus, in a company that has a BBQ culture, any strategy that is built to move the company forward will by default include a strategy that uses Quality behaviors of CPI as one of the tools to bring improved results to the bottom line.

My good friend Terry Mathis is the CEO of one of the nation's top Behavior Based Safety (BBS) consulting companies, ProAct Safety. In one of his recent books, *Inside Strategy,* he and his partner, Shawn Galloway, talk about value creation from within an organization. The term they use for this, as you might guess, is inside strategy. The inside strategy is flowed down to every department and becomes the cultural imperative that supports the goals of the company. This is one of my favorite quotes from their book.

"By contrast, the inside strategy is a framework of choices organizations make to determine and deliver value. Inside and outside strategies are part of a whole. Behavior is dependent on what you want to achieve. Yet it is surprising how often this seemingly obvious idea can be forgotten. When conditions change, you need to question if your approach still makes sense."[1]

[1] *Inside Strategy: Value Creation from Within Your Organization,* Shawn Galloway and Terry Mathis, SCE Press, 2016.

Often companies are stuck and unwilling to change strategy when market conditions impact their business. It may seem intuitively obvious that this is a flawed behavior, yet companies stick to their plans as though that would make everything better. Anyone who has been in the military understands that this is how battles are lost. We must remain flexible with our strategies and adapt as situations change over time. We must always have a plan B; in highly complex or competitive markets, a plan C would be prudent. The AOP mentioned in the case study above never had a plan B. When market conditions changed, such as a competitor winning a bid that we had expected to come our way, there was no contingency plan in place. A scramble occurred to compensate, and this often had a negative impact on other plans there were in place. Business is a chess game; without a strategy including alternate plays, the game may be lost. Most companies operating "by the seat of their pants" will not achieve long-term sustainable positive results.

Takeaway for this chapter: *The reason for a company's existence is value creation. Value cannot be created within a company without a strategy pointing to where you want to be in years to come. Included in that strategy should be the identification of barriers to success at all levels and the development a plan for how to move around and/or overcome those barriers. Achieving the success you desire requires an understanding of the barriers and includes a remediation plan. This is the strategy that you will deploy. Strategy is not just the set of top-level objectives. To be achievable, it must be translated into a strategy applicable to every department in a company. When we start thinking about barriers to Quality success in engineering, marketing, finance, or other departments, the strategy for Quality involves removing those barriers and creating more value within the department. A successful strategy deployment occurs when the top-level strategy is cascaded down into the organization so that every department understands the objectives and has developed its own departmental strategy that is tied to and contributes to the top-level objective. When every department and every employee understands that they have a part in the success of the company through the strategy contribution, then the company is evolving to a culture of Behavior Based Quality (BBQ). This is how sustainable value is created.*

5

Getting Started on Your BBQ Journey

The first four chapters of this book should have made you aware that accountability for Quality should be part of every organization in your company. Moreover, a strategy for Quality that supports the company's growth and long-term objective should flow through every department. In this chapter we will discuss how to communicate the message to amplify Quality awareness, explain how to build metrics using a style of key performance indicators (KPI) that drive change, and then look at cascading objectives and strategic task metrics into the organization. The balance of the book will continue to develop your thinking around CPI (compliance, prevention, and improvement) behaviors in concert with supporting various tools and methods to build or transform organizations to achieve a culture of Behavior Based Quality (BBQ) that drives sustainable positive change and results to your financial bottom line.

I hope you have been lucky enough to work for companies that have a modern perspective of CPI-based Quality. If so, you will have seen examples set by executives you worked with that have become part of your management tool belt. On the other hand, it's conceivable that you progressed in your career in companies that did not have the Behavior Based Quality (BBQ) culture that I am promoting in this book. You are likely aware of Quality, but you may have always thought it was what goes on in the factory or the service department. The set of Quality behaviors may never have made it off the factory floor or past the manufacturing or operations manager. If this is the case, I hope that your perspective will have broadened by the time you finish this book, allowing you to think outside the box and acknowledge that Quality behaviors belong everywhere in your company. When you believe this, then you are on your way to understanding the importance of a BBQ culture focused on CPI, it's cornerstone, to achieve sustainable results.

Your path to success starts with *you*! Sure, you've heard this before. You didn't rise to this level of management by accident. You rose because you made yourself stand out as a positive contributor, a leader, someone bright and intelligent who can be trusted. Most of us are put in positions we earn by working hard and demonstrating our abilities to succeed in the assigned task. Because you have been the purveyor of your growth and success, this should not be a hard concept to grasp. Along the way you have held leadership positions, some of which were not comfortable. The discomfort may have come from inexperience, from unfamiliarity with a particular subject matter space, or even from dealing with new people that you work for or manage. You may have been uncomfortable dealing with people in your first management job, in particular with performance reviews, task assignments, strategic objectives, and goal setting. Most challenging of all is dealing with poor performance. Needless to say, you deal with these challenges professionally and eventually learn to handle them with ease.

A person advancing in a career without proper training and an understanding of business functions—including Quality tools, behaviors, and actions—may very well lack the fundamental abilities to effectively lead or recognize the value of a move to a culture of Quality. The intent of this book so far has been to provide an executive or manager unfamiliar with Quality with a basic understanding of why Quality is important and the value that a culture of Quality can bring to a company's bottom-line financials. For those in Quality management being called on to "keep things in order," this book is intended to add to your knowledge, allowing you to effectively facilitate an executive's understanding of the value of a cultural transformation to BBQ supported by the behaviors of CPI.

Most executives come up through the ranks of sales, finance, or engineering. They may even have experience in more than one of these functional areas. Generally, these functions are not operationally engaged in Quality practices or philosophies. It is not often that we see executives who grow out of an operations background, where there is usually more of an operational engagement and awareness of Quality practices and philosophies. Consequently, most executives are not well suited to drive change through development and implementation of a culture of Quality. Relying on the Quality management team to "keep things in order" does not usually bring awareness of the positive impact of a culture of BBQ.

I'll wager that throughout your career, except for a few really good bosses or associates who either mentored you or set a great example, you have looked at other managers and felt that you could do better if you had their job. Taking a positive approach to this line of thinking, I don't consider this job-envy by any means; rather, it's an exercise in mental gymnastics. If you had that job, you would do it this way or that way, or you would recognize the positive attributes of what that manager is doing and consider that style, behavior, or approach as part of your toolbelt of learnings. You may have had similar thoughts about managers, senior managers, vice presidents, COOs, or even CEOs. Now you are in one of those positions and you want to do the best job you can. What are you doing about it?

Will you "keep on keeping on," getting along to stay employed by not making waves? Think about this: Sailing on calm waters does not provide any lessons on how to sail in troubled seas. Many of these "get along to stay employed" manager types rise in an organization, sometimes to those lofty positions, but generally they reach a level where they are ill prepared to make necessary strategic decisions because they have not taken risks and learned from their successes or failures. Dr. Laurence J. Peter and Raymond Hull wrote about this in *The Peter Principle* (1969). Simply getting along does not create great experience that is needed to become a great leader. Leadership is about being brave and doing what is best for the company and its people. This is just part of your path to success.

Case Study

While working in the oil and gas industry for a subsea well head manufacturer, I had the good fortune to work with one of the bravest executives I had ever known. During his tenure as CEO, he had become a believer in the BBQ tenets of compliance, prevention, and improvement. In this position he was instrumental in guiding and supporting a cultural change that embraced BBQ. During a business downturn, he realized he needed to take action to reduce costs. As often is typical in these situations, his first action was to get rid of the "deadwood," the poor performers. His second action, and here is the brave part, was to resist the conventional wisdom that called for looking deeper into the organization to make additional cuts. Instead, he reassigned excess staff to critical improvement projects that reduced operating costs, improved designs, and built a strategy that virtually killed the competition when the market turned around. This company came out of the downturn faster and more efficient than its competitors. That executive took a risk by believing in his employees' ability to take advantage of the situation and create positive results. He put excess resources to good use by maintaining their employment through a tough time. This level of bravery is seldom seen at executive levels because it contradicts the normal conventions of what executives and their board of directors believe they should do during market downturns. It is a tough decision to make, harder because nobody can be sure of how long the downturn will last. The option of reducing workforce is always open, but brave decision making can bring about savings that financially eclipse what can be achieved by cutting back on staff.

By now you are asking what this has to do with Quality. It has *everything* to do with Quality! As I have stated throughout this book, Quality is a behavior. Part of that behavior calls for doing the right thing under tough situations to achieve the best results. As an executive, you want to come out of tough situations in better shape than when you entered them. You want to recover faster and better than your competition. Understanding and adopting a culture of Quality will allow you to do just that if you give it a chance.

As the executive leader, *you* will be setting the pace for behaviors that will translate directly to, and become the culture of, the company. How *you* promote, support, lead by example, and insist on adhering to those CPI-based behaviors will set the course for your company.

What if you are not yet an executive? Don't wait until you attain that executive position to be brave. The same holds true for managers. Start leading by example today and carry those behaviors with you as you grow your career. Those behaviors are far more likely to provide positive visibility than the "getting along" behaviors.

Okay, so we have talked about the high-level behaviors. How do you know what needs to be addressed with your newly found or reinvigorated understanding of Quality behaviors? Remember when we talked about thinking you could do someone else's job better? Well, now it's your turn.

Mapping the path

It is time to get you started on your path to success now that some of the foundational behaviors have been established for a CPI-based Quality culture. Your path to success has everything to do with Quality and the points I have made from the Preface to the end of Chapter 4. The rest of this book continues to focus on Quality as the objective, but gives you some "how to" guidance that will help you on your journey. Before you react with direct action, I'd recommend that you assess the "landscape" of your company to see what is working and what can be improved. From there, establish a plan for what you will do and for how and where you will start.

Whether you are starting from scratch, building a company that has no foundation of Quality culture, or bringing change to a company with a basic understanding of Quality, my strongest recommendation is to avoid jumping directly into metrics. Metrics will give you an understanding of current performance levels, but may start the cultural transformation off on the wrong direction. Instead, communicate to your executive staff your intent to build a CPI-based culture of Quality. Then progress into a series of cross functional Quality awareness training sessions that will reach every employee. I prefer small groups of 10-35 people to encourage dialog between attendees and the facilitator. It should be clear to employees that you are setting the pace for the company to follow. Facilitation and training may be accomplished by internal or consulting subject matter experts, but it is you who set the objective by supporting the cultural transformation. To change or improve Quality in any process output, it's essential that the leader first establish and promote the foundation of right behaviors.

Once the behaviors have been communicated and understood, move into the Quality philosophy. "You can't change what you don't measure." This will set the stage for your team to consider areas of suspected poor performance or waste reduction opportunities and follow those up by prioritizing improvement opportunities.

Now it's time for metrics

Once these improvement opportunities are established, the team can move on to define a set of metrics that properly reports performance of the target area or process. First, let's talk about what I call the style of metrics. This simply boils down to the measurement of cause or effect. Here's an example: *If you are building widgets and your target is 100 widgets per day and your output is 90 per day, it's what I would call an effect metric. If, in the same example, you were measuring the barriers to achieve 100 widgets per day, this would be a cause metric.* Which one do you think will drive more effective change?

Using effect metrics is the easiest approach to take, and it's a trap people fall into when they implement metrics without thought to whether the right things are being measured or whether the metric will actually drive change. More important, if the reason for measurement and change is not supported by a foundation of cultural behaviors, the value of the metrics will not be sustainable over time. In a culture of Quality, the cause metric will provide details that "jump out at you" for easy visual recognition and thus provide the path to corrective action through prevention and improvement.

If your company already has some metrics in place, the first questions to ask yourself has to do with whether they measure what you think should be changed. The next question has to do with timeliness of metrics. Are they routinely updated? Or are they just pretty pictures on the wall that have been out of date for weeks or months, providing no current value? Are the metrics actionable? In other words, do the metrics measure cause or effect? If things are "wonky," can a root cause be determined from the data with little or no deep dive into analysis to take corrective action? In Figure 5, the top chart gives no clue as to why the throughput to close monthly financials is as high as it is nor why the performance is approaching its target.

Financial Closing Performance

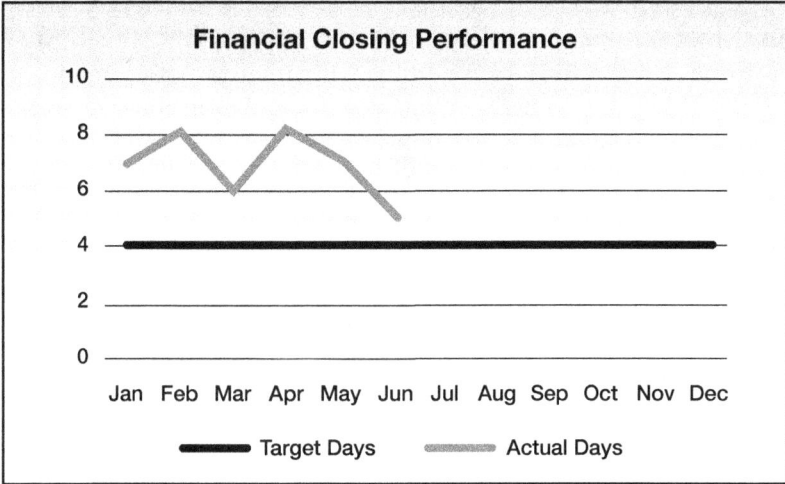

Effect Metric

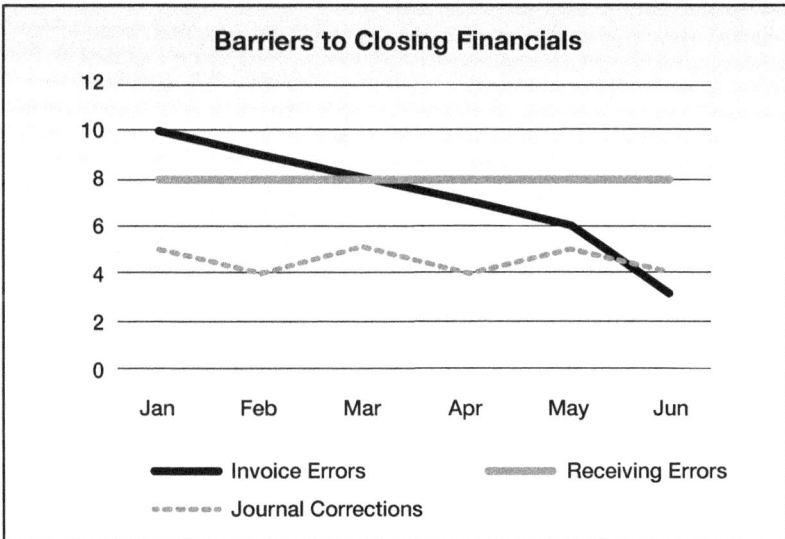

Barriers to Closing Financials

Cause Metric

Figure 5 Effect and cause metrics for financial closing performance.

The bottom chart in Figure 5 shows three barriers to closing (cause) that are being tracked. It would appear that something has been implemented to improve invoice errors. Journal corrections are erratic, leading one to believe that nothing is being done to improve this area. It would seem clear that nothing is being done to improve receiving errors; there is no improvement shown. The two metrics together tell a story, but the "cause" metric is actually giving reason to the effect metric; it also indicates areas needing focused corrective action through prevention and improvement. Cause metrics make the best key performance indicators (KPIs); these are the ones that define barriers to success. Therefore the solution that brings improvement goes directly to the bottom line. This is further enhanced for visible impact when the metric is monetized.

Many companies use only effect metrics and wonder why performance does not improve. The manager says, "We have to improve the month-end closing cycle." That's great leadership, isn't it? Who is "we"? Who has accountability? Using an effect metric tells you only that things are not so good. This is why most metrics fail. If you believe metrics do not exist to measure the right stuff, build ones that consider cause of performance; then track the measurement for a period of time so that you can confirm or deny your suspicions. Chances are, other opportunities will show themselves with a closer level of scrutiny.

Here's a clue: Most poor performing processes stem from input and output *requirements* for one or more process steps not being properly defined or met. Recall our discussion on *compliance* in Chapter 1? People tend to focus on the "end state" output requirement (for example, complete monthly financial closing, with a performance metric of four days). Yet, there are hundreds of process steps that must be completed successfully without error in order for the financials to close in less than four days. These steps may cross multiple department boundaries and involve numerous process owners. Thus, it is important to understand whether the performance metric being tracked is for the end state (effect), or whether success is measured by each department's interaction to the end state (cause). True end state improvement will not be sustainable if you don't focus on the process steps creating non-conformances or delays. In Six Sigma language, that's waste. Waste is unanticipated (and generally non-recoverable) cost related to errors, failures, non-conformances, time delays, excess material to cover failures, and… Well, you get the picture.

In a company with a BBQ culture of CPI, the method to improve performance starts with one person at the top (you) supporting and setting the pace while promoting cause metrics for team implementation. This is how sustainable change is achieved.

Side Note: *Six Sigma (6σ) performance is equal to 3.4 defects per one million opportunities for failure or 99.999999% acceptance. Six Sigma was once thought of as the "holy grail" of Quality performance in high-volume repetitive manufacturing such as integrated circuits and pharmaceuticals. These industries are now operating in excess of 11 Sigma of Quality performance. When considering the impact of failure in these industries, one can understand why improvement is a business imperative.*

When you start collecting metrics at the process step level, they most always will be of the "cause" type. When these metrics are used to reduce or eliminate (prevent) the cause of errors (non-conformances), the path is set to achieve sustainable results.

If you collect data for cause metrics, ask yourself these questions. Are they recent and up to date? Are the metrics being reviewed at the appropriate level of management? Are actions assigned and tracked to assure corrective action or improvement is occurring? If the answer to these questions sparks uncertainty, then the leadership may want to reconsider the effectiveness of its Quality transformation or consider the need for a cultural Quality transformation initiative if the culture of Quality is lacking or waning. This takes us back to our first chapter and the question: "Where are *you* on your Quality journey?"

What is a SMART metric?

We've talked a lot about "cause" metrics, but that term has a wide range of possibilities. Establishing good metrics is a lot like setting departmental or company objectives. There is a standard about setting SMART objectives that is almost universally understood. I believe the same approach is applicable to setting SMART metrics. SMART metrics are defined as: **S**pecific (strategic), **M**easurable, **A**ccurate (attainable or achievable), **R**eliable (realistic or relevant), and **T**imely.

It's challenging to determine measurable and achievable metrics. Often what is measurable is not realistically achievable. For example, let's say we want a Six Sigma level of service availability from our network server (that's 99.999% availability). What are the requirements? Is the service to be available 7/24/365? If so, that would leave about five minutes per year for preventive maintenance. This measurement is destined to reflect a missed target when performing a monthly half hour preventive maintenance regimen. Moreover, the metric would seem to be effect-based and highly unlikely to be achievable. This takes us back to the question of setting requirements and asking whether we are measuring the right thing for the right reason. Perhaps a better metric would be service availability between the working hours of 8:00 a.m. and 6:00 p.m., five days a week. Then track the items that prevent that service level from being met (e.g., power outage for two hours, component failure of one hour). These measures are cause-based, time sensitive, measurable, and actionable.

In a culture of Quality we want to tie metrics to objectives as well as performance indicators. The SMART approach supports both. Technically, one could say that measuring process non-conformances is as much about performance as it is about measuring ongoing status to cascaded company objectives. One may be related to the cost impact of failure, the other to improvement initiatives that prevent waste by improving a process. There is a fine line here where issues sometimes become confused. Although we must always support prevention initiatives to take process failures to zero, often in the interest of process improvement a Lean initiative will improve a process before it has been rendered defect free. The resulting "improvement" is that we are churning out bad parts faster and cheaper. We are still generating defects in the process, even though we have improved the process to build 150 per hour versus the unimproved process that was only building 100 per hour. If the defect rate prior to improvement was 10% and we did nothing to improve the cause of the defects, we are still generating 10% defects, but now 50% more of them. If the process saved $100 per hour in processing time and it costs $10 to correct a reject, the math would indicate that we have moved from $100 reject cost per hour to $150 reject cost per hour. Our improvement actually resulted in $50 of additional reject costs. I hope this example will encourage you to have your team use "cause" metrics to identify issues and install prevention measures as part of corrective action before moving on to improve a process that is generating defects.

Everyone has a contribution

I sneaked a word in above: cascaded objectives. For the owners, executives, or department managers, remember this starts with you at the top. In a culture of BBQ, you guide your team to set objectives for the company to improve profit from X dollars to Y dollars in the current fiscal year, improve on time delivery (OTD) from X to Y in the next six months, and so on. These are high-level objectives that you want to cascade down to departments within your organization. Typically, Sales might be challenged to increase revenue so that the increased receipts by nature of volume will increase the dollar amount of profit (was this a SMART objective?). If Sales and Marketing were the only groups tasked with this objective, this would be a targeted objective rather than a cascaded objective. What are we measuring, sales growth or profit increase? What about a metric of increased profit as a percent of sales from X to Y by Q4? A cascaded objective is one that is flowed down into the organization, where every department that can make a contribution to increased profit dollars takes on a lower-tiered objective that supports the top-level objective. In this approach, Sales and Marketing has an objective, Engineering will be tasked with taking out excessive cost in the product design, Manufacturing will be tasked with taking waste out of processes, Finance may be tasked with finding a tax incentive that will contribute more dollars to the bottom line, and so on. These lower-level objectives all support the top-level objective of improving profit from X to Y. This cascading should go as deep as possible into every department until a contribution to the next level up can no longer be made.

I have seen many companies set annual objectives around profit dollars, margin percentage, delivery, and more, yet these are never translated directly down into all of the possible contributors of those measures in the company. Thus, Engineering may never be asked to look into its existing designs to remove excess cost of materials, labor, functionality, or even time span from product concept to product delivery. Cascading objectives from the top down into the organization is a CPI behavior that is part of a culture of Quality.

Example of a cascading process

A number of tools are available to help with the behavior of cascading objectives down into an organization. The tool that I believe provides the best visual indication of cascading is a Hoisin-based format that often is referred to as strategic deployment process (SDP). This tool requires the developers (i.e., the executive team) to first define no more than six three-year to five-year break-out objectives in prioritized order of importance. Think about this. How will your company successfully grow or remain competitive if you don't have a plan? Moreover, why shouldn't your entire management team be involved in plan development and participate in success by understanding the details of the strategic plan? When the three-year to five-year strategic plan is completed, the executive team moves on to establish objectives to be put in place in the next fiscal year (plan year) that supports achieving the three-year to five-year plan.

Note: This type of planning usually takes place several months prior to the start of the next fiscal year; at that point plans, objectives, and measures for success are defined, set, and ready to measure from day one.

The plan-year objectives must consist of at least one and no more than five objectives (ideally three) supporting each of the long-term plan objectives. These should be ranked in prioritized order. This set of strategic and plan-year objectives would most likely be presented to and approved by the board of directors. When the plan-year objectives are approved and assured to support attainment of the long-term plan, the next step is to define strategic tasks for each department capable of contributing to achieving each of the objectives. These tasks should typically number no more than three per plan-year objective for each of first tier of management.

Note: The reason for this is that the number of tasks will increase as the objectives are further cascaded down into the organization. Keeping these prioritized, targeted, and few in number at the top keeps objectives from becoming overwhelming and unachievable as they are cascaded into the organization.

These strategic tasks or initiatives must be vetted to assure that they contribute positive impact to accomplish the related plan-year objectives. Once this is done, we start the cascading process down into the next layer of management by building a matrix of each department that is expected to contribute to the identified initiatives. Although not in Hoisin format, the example below shows the progression of objectives from the long-range plan down to the current year owner of a strategic initiative.

- **3- to 5-year breakout objective #1**
  - ☐ Capture dominance in market share from 35% to greater than 55%
  - **Plan year supporting objective #1**
    - ☐ Reduce time to market
    - **Strategic supporting task (engineering department)**
      - ☐ Improve engineering development time
      - **Measure of success**
        - ☐ Improve design cycle time from 356 days to 120 days by December [plan year]
          - **Owner: engineering director**
    - **Strategic supporting task (marketing department)**
      - ☐ Increase valve product advertising
      - **Measure of success**
        - ☐ Increase advertising in energy sector from X$ to Y$ by December [plan year]
          - **Owner: marketing director**
- **3- to 5-year breakout objective #2**
  - ☐ Increase Profit Margin from 5% EBIT to 18% EBIT
  - **Plan year supporting objective #2**
    - ☐ And so on similar to above example above for each department

I believe that you will agree that this approach meets the requirements of a SMART objective process. Most importantly, the objective is cascaded down into the organization to all contributing organizational teams.

In the previous example, the engineering director will cascade "improve engineering development time" to his or her department managers who can contribute to reducing design cycle time with another level of supporting objective(s) following the same format. In this example, a drafting manager, a reliability manager, and a design manager may each be tasked with contributing to cycle time reduction in the functions they manage.

The pace and direction that you set by these cascaded objectives is then maintained by a discipline process of routine and timely review, where your executive team meets with their direct reports (preferably monthly and usually as a group) and goes over the status of the metrics that measure success to the current year strategic plan. It is impossible for me to imagine that a disciplined process of review will not uncover areas of waste and non-conformances that will lead to corrective action. These will make a positive impact to the strategic objectives and thus the long-term objectives as well. It's likely there will be lower-level metrics as well that will identify opportunities for improvement.

Why so much focus on cascaded objectives?

I have spent so much time in this chapter on cascaded objectives because I believe it is important that the executive leader provide guidance and set the pace for a culture of Quality. When we go back to our definition of Quality as CPI, the strategic deployment process provides one of the best tools available to identify and set a path for improvement that will be Quality based through the behaviors of CPI. This, of course, is only one of the tools in the arsenal that supports sustainable bottom-line results through the behaviors of CPI.

Note: *If you are interested in more detailed information on the strategic deployment process, you will find numerous references using your favorite browser and search engine. Training is also provided by the author of this book.*

Takeaway for this chapter: *The path to success relies on your understanding of Quality behaviors and of how to translate and incorporate them into the fabric and DNA of the company. Behaviors that drive bottom-line results will be reinforced when you and your team are aligned on long- and short-term objectives. Objectives can be initiated through the strategic planning of your company's long-term goals. These goals are then supported by near-term objectives that are cascaded down into your organization to each department. Timely performance measurement to these objectives provides the information needed to take corrective actions in areas needing improvement; that is rendered through CPI (compliance, prevention, and improvement) behaviors. Adherence to these behaviors promotes a culture of Quality that brings sustainable results to each department's performance and thus to the bottom line of the company. None of this is sustainable without a foundation of strategic planning or discipline of timely measurement and management engagement taking place to track progress.*

6

Setting Requirements
for Your Objectives

*Getting started on your cultural transformation to
Behavior Based Quality (BBQ) requires embracing compliance,
prevention, and improvement (CPI) as the basis for change
and achieving sustainable results. Achieving sustainable
results depends upon how well you understand and implement
requirements. Establishing agreed-upon requirements between
supplier and customer (internal or external) is the key to
prevention. There are many Quality-based tools to help you
with this process. Pick the one that works for your company by
keeping in mind that setting agreed-upon requirements is the
basis for performance measurement.*

Okay, so what is the first thing that you will do to make a difference with your new updated knowledge of CPI-driven Behavior Based Quality (BBQ) culture? Your new path to Quality starts with defining a strategy and then setting high-level objectives that are cascaded down into each region, division, and department within the company. Those objectives are supported by tasks with associated key performance indicators (KPIs) that track the achievement to each department's objectives. Frequent and routine schedule of reviews are established to assess performance to the metrics that define success and achievement to those objectives. Sounds great, doesn't it?

I'd like to say that you have "arrived," but there is one more very important aspect to address to assure success. Success in a BBQ culture of CPI can only be achieved by highlighting and focusing on the *prevention* aspect of CPI. *Compliance* will bring you to the point of meeting industry standards and customer requirements. *Improvement* will bring about positive change to process, design, and/or services. It is prevention that drives and sustains success in the "C," "P," and "I" sectors of a BBQ culture. Here is why: Compliance is about conforming to mutually agreed-upon requirements. True improvement cannot happen unless there is conformance to requirements. Prevention cannot be established unless requirements are met. Therefore, setting requirements properly is the most important aspect of prevention.

Setting requirements

The excited teenage boy said to his friend, "I want a red car that goes fast!" Pretty simple requirements, which could result in anything from a Ferrari to a 1953 Oldsmobile with a "souped-up" engine (my first car). The teenager's "want" leaves out many lower-level requirements that are a necessity to affirm the teenager's ability to fulfill his dream.

In business we often under specify the requirements of what we want as well. Consider the objective from your manager: "We need to reduce cost." A blanket statement such as this may lead to months of effort in an area that brings about little to no improvement, while areas of offering great opportunity go unnoticed.

Often we think of requirements as defined by the end deliverable (e.g., pay invoices). The fact of the matter is that the steps leading up to the end deliverable (pay invoices) have unique input and output requirements that must be met in order to achieve flawless execution of the final requirement (pay invoice).

There are many ways to approach setting proper top- and lower-level requirements that bring about positive results. A seasoned manager should be experienced in doing this, or at the very least know what she or he doesn't know and bring in experts to work through the process of establishing requirements that will ultimately bring about zero non-conformities. You will find that setting proper requirements will translate to lower cost and faster processing time.

Figure 6 illustrates the process steps needed to produce an output. If the output of the process noted by the yellow circle is "pay invoices," the six process steps (1-6) indicate the various actions that take place between one process operator and the next in line to complete the final output. Processes are often defined by their final output, in this example "pay invoices." With a focus on end state requirements, this may leave individual process steps without defined requirements. If all six process steps have an unclear set of individual requirements, how can one be assured that the end state requirement will be met with zero non-conformance or zero waste? The lack of specifics and clarity creates waste and non-conformances within the process chain that often impact the final output.

It's important to know that each process step has its own individual requirements that support the next process step. Each process step's input and output has its own unique set of requirements that must be met in order to properly complete the operation and move on to the next step of the process. This is depicted in Figure 6 by the expansion of process step #3 into what is called the SIPOC model. The term SIPOC stands for **S**upplier-**I**nput-**P**rocess-**O**utput-**C**ustomer. In this example, process step #4 is the customer of process step #3, which has a supplier that is process step #2. In order for the customer at process step #4 to receive the output from process step #3 as its input, all requirements for process step #3 must be met. This continues for the entire chain of process steps including the final output. If requirements are properly established at each step and all environmental issues of training, instruction, tools, equipment, and facilities have been met, then each process step should produce zero non-conformances. The key is determining the requirements that are appropriate for the process step. If the name for process step #3 is "deliver invoices," you can see that this could be too general and indicate any specific requirement other than the deliverable. Thus, the more specific requirement in order to complete the "deliver invoices"

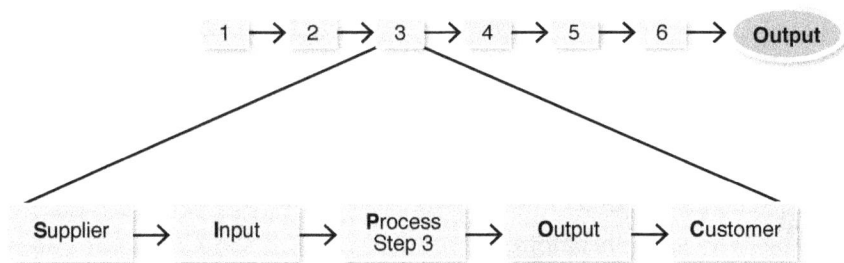

Figure 6   Process steps needed to produce an output.

process correctly would be as follows: 1) Compile list of open service supplier invoices; plus, 2) list shall be all invoices open as of the last day of the previous month; plus, 3) list shall be provided to accounts payable by the third working day of each month. Note that I have used three output requirements to define the deliverable from process step #3. While the single output is still "deliver invoices," the requirements to achieve this provides clear direction on what is expected to meet the input requirements of the next process step.

Note: *In naming the process step in the example above I used only two words, a verb and noun. Here's the hard part when mapping a process and establishing requirements: If it takes more than a single verb and noun to describe a process step, you have not yet parsed that process step into its smallest or individual elements. Failing to "scope down" to this level of brevity will render it nearly impossible to set the proper requirements for the proper process owner.*

Without fail, issues that arise out of a process, whether non-conformances, excessive processing time, or other forms of waste, can be attributed to two key impact areas: 1) unclear or lacking requirements, and 2) poorly or inadequately addressed environmental necessities of a) training, b) instructions, c) tools, and d) facility requirements (i.e., lighting, air conditioning, and so on).

It is extremely important to establish requirements for process steps as well as environmental necessities. This is the core principle of *prevention*. If this is not attended to properly, then the *improvement* portion of Quality culture will likely never be fully realized nor achieve sustainability as a cultural imperative.

As easy as it sounds, setting requirements is one of the hardest and most time-consuming actions that are taken when you set yourself upon the journey of a Quality cultural transformation, especially when you are taking existing processes with defects to a state of zero non-conformances. Establishing new processes is easier because you are starting with a fresh palette of opportunities. If your company does not have a department devoted to excellence in business processes, with people who have adopted the thinking and behaviors proposed in this book, then it may be prudent to bring in professional outside resources to assist with the training and cultural transformation to get you and your team started on the correct path.

Takeaway for this chapter: *The root of compliance, prevention, and improvement (CPI) Behavior Based Quality (BBQ) culture is the establishment of input and output requirement for all process steps. These must be mutually agreed upon between process step owner, internal or external supplier, and customer. Compliance to these requirements brings about prevention. Once prevention is achieved, processes can be improved to remove waste, thus improving cost. The SIPOC model is one tool that seems to have universal appeal in that it forces one to look into the details of each process step. If you are not pleased with the results that you are achieving in your current Quality performance or process improvement, it's time to think outside the box and get professional support from someone who can help you define requirements that prevent non-conformances and improve processes through a culture of BBQ.*

7

Setting Achievable Objective Tasks

We talked a great deal in the previous chapter about the process of establishing short- and long-term objectives and using a tool to cascade them into the organization. Other than by shear inertia, it is doubtful that a company will progress if objectives are not set—and even more doubtful it will progress if objectives are not measured in a SMART manner.

M any small companies do not take the time to establish goals for where they want to be in three to five years, let alone in the current year. If goals are not set and progress measured, the company is treading water and moving nowhere. Equally damaging are shot-term goals that are not aligned with the long-term goal. Imagine a company setting a five-year objective of increasing sales by 25% each year, and then setting a current-year objective of doubling profit. Both seem like positive objectives, but does doubling profit support a 25% sales increase if the price of the product is increased or the number of engineers and sales people is reduced to achieve the current-year goal? As silly as it sounds, this is too frequently the case in corporate America. The same level of disconnect can often be seen down into the organization when departments are attempting to set supporting goals for current and long-term corporate objectives. These are some of the traps that people fall into when trying to establish meaningful objectives that set the pace for the company as it moves from year to year.

Another typical trap is encountered when a company wants it all…now! The trap is sprung when there are too many objectives, so many that the lines blur between long- and short-term objectives; they appear to be the same. This creates confusion about what is most important to address and when. Another problem with wanting it all now is that objectives mandated by management can be so excessive that there are not enough resources to properly address all of them. This, of course, creates more confusion about priorities that need to be addressed and in what order. This trap has no prejudice between large or small companies. Poor leadership can exist anywhere. I hope that reading this book and understanding its examples will help you to understand the importance of working on the vital few versus the trivial many.

Focus, focus, focus

Achieving great success on a few key prioritized objectives is far more rewarding than spreading resources too thin and achieving mediocre results across a broad spectrum. More important, recognition from the smaller number of successes has a greater impact on morale as well as on the financial bottom line. The key here is to focus on near-term objectives that support the longer-term goals of the company. For many reasons, it may be necessary to readjust the near or long-term objectives periodically to maintain balance with the dynamics and trends of the market you work within. Think of the classic example of Sony making the first video recording and playback machine called BetaMax. Although Sony had a superior product, it was expensive and they lost out to the lower-cost VHS technology that quickly put Sony out of the BetaMax business. Then companies making VHS video machines were eclipsed by the introduction of first DVDs and then Blue-ray technology (led by Sony, which had learned its lesson). Today the trend is to online streaming devices from new market leaders such as Roku, Amazon, Netflix, and others. Evolution or extinction; that really is the way of things and you need to be aware.

The last paragraph has dealt more with the intent of this chapter's title: Setting Achievable Objective Tasks. The reason for the build-up is to emphasize the process of establishing supportive goals and cascading them down into the organization using the strategic deployment tool described in the previous chapter. What we didn't go into deeply in that chapter was the establishment of tasks supporting objectives (by department) and how to measure success. Without going back and going into further detail on how to use the tool, the issue at hand is to define a metric that establishes the change as "improve Z from X to Y by a date" (e.g., improve first-pass yield of product A testing from 90% to 95% by [date in current year]). Do you see how this sets a specific measurement versus simply stating "improve first-pass test yield by 10%"? Which is a more concrete measure that will drive improvement when reviewed on a scheduled basis? If your company builds ten products and product A is the most costly in terms of Quality reject rate, taking a prioritized, focused approach puts your resources to work on the area of greatest impact.

Let's take this a step further. If your company manufactures ten products and you put your resources to work on improving Quality in each of them, do you think you will achieve the same impactful results in the same amount of time? The point here is to prioritize issues from greatest impact to lowest and address them in that order with available resources, still allowing the "day job" to get done. Remember, running the process *is* the day job. Fixing the process impacts getting the day job done; trying to fix too many things at one time will stall momentum. Improving high-impact issues creates a success pattern that allows you and your team to rejoice in success and creates positive momentum that will carry through to the next success.

Is this Quality culture?

This approach should further emphasize the positive impact of cascading objectives down to each department in order to define tasks that support the next level up with tasks and metrics that measure success. If you are asking how this supports a culture of Quality, consider that CPI: 1) is the definition of the function of Quality, and 2) is the basis for change. The discipline of maintaining this process associated with frequent reviews (see below) is the demonstration of management's commitment to Quality as a cultural imperative.

Now the kicker. To be successful in achieving your annual objectives, it's necessary to review the measures of success supporting them on a regular basis (e.g., monthly); that demonstrates management support and belief in the objectives. Moreover, the metrics that you use to measure success must be identified by the period of review frequency (e.g., monthly). In other words, as in our example above, if we are to achieve an improvement in product A testing yield in four months, the target yield indicating improvement must be identified in each month. (e.g., January 90%, February 92%, March 94%, and April 95%). In this manner, each month's progress is measured and accounted for. Thus, there are no surprises at the end of the measurement period, as there would be if the only measure displayed was the future state of the last month of April. By using this approach, success can be celebrated upon achieving each month's goal. When the goal is not achieved, then the owner of the process should present to the management review team the causes of the miss, the corrective actions that are being taken to get back on track, and an estimate of how long it will take to get back on track.

To be really successful with this process, the management review team must exist at a high enough level in the company to assure that task and metric owners understand that they are being held accountable during the review process for performance to objectives and any related corrective action to bring errant measures back on track. In medium-sized companies, this often is the CEO or COO. In very large companies, this may be delegated down to the general manager level, who will report back up the chain of command on group performance to cascaded objectives set from the top. Making this a disciplined but positive and frequent review process is a vitally important part of driving positive change.

Remember: *Accountability is one of the behaviors associated with CPI.*

As you move through the process of setting and measuring cascaded objectives, the prevention and improvement behaviors of your Quality culture will strengthen. Lower-level metrics will be developed that measure process performance. This is likely where you will find the data that will provide the answers to root causes of poor performance to cascaded objectives.

Takeaway for this chapter: *Establishing proper long-term company goals that are supported by near-term or current-year objectives that are purposefully cascaded down into the company's infrastructure is the foundation for growth and improvement. Measuring performance to objectives that are specific, measurable, achievable, realistic, and time based is where behavior and actions tie together to cause Quality improvement and the growth of a Behavior Based Quality (BBQ) culture focused on compliance, prevention, and improvement (CPI). Adopting CPI as the focus is the primary ingredient of a BBQ culture.*

8

Start Finding
Those Hidden Profits

As people perform processes day in and day out, the familiarity of it all may actually be masking real tangible opportunities for improvement. Acceptance of what has become the "norm" may be robbing you of unaccounted profits. It's time to think outside the box and look deeper into the processes in your business for those hidden profits.

You are probably saying, "What hidden profits? I know every square foot of my facility and all that goes on. If anything were hidden, I'd know about it." Hold on a moment. Did you add the cost of inspection, scrap, or rework in your product pricing? You might respond, "Of course I add labor cost for inspection." Whereupon I would ask: Do you add labor cost for the additional inspection required to inspect rework after the first or subsequent rejections for non-conformances? Would you answer, "Well, not exactly. I calculated the entire cost of inspection labor last year then divided by the total assembly labor to get a percent of inspection labor that I add to the costing formula." This is the perfect example of hidden profits that are found in what some people call the hidden factory. You have counted for multiple inspections (and repair) that should not occur if you had a factory running without non-conformances. Moreover, you are pricing defects into the cost of your product and are potentially losing business (due to price and maybe delayed delivery) to competition that is operating more efficiently than you are.

Put more simply, the hidden factory is any extraordinary cost or waste that is not accounted for in standard cost of product or service pricing. This simple definition of hidden factory should also account for opportunity cost of creating an improved process through Lean initiatives or other tools of process improvement. Figure 7 illustrates examples of a process as designed and how it may have grown over the years with additional "required" steps to keep product rolling efficiently.

When prevention is incorporated into the process and then reviewed for improvement, the possible flow is potentially two fewer steps.

"Overhead," or what is often called burden costs, often hide elements of the hidden factory. Cost of poor Quality (COPQ) is also part of this. Companies typically do not, or may not realize that they do, build scrap and/or rework into their product cost model. Imagine the surprise to the factory manager when she looks deeper into what poor Quality is actually costing her. The actual process to create the product versus the process as designed is littered with opportunity for improvement in both flow and Quality through elimination of waste and non-conformances. If you consider that each of the black diamonds in Figure 7 represents an inspection operation necessitated by demonstrated poor Quality, the black rectangles represent additional steps (labor and material) needed in the process to bring the product back into conformance. The black diamonds and the black rectangles represent additional cost from the hidden factory that are typically not (knowingly) built into the cost of the product, but impact operating costs and profit margins directly. Consider that a process without defects would eliminate the need for in-process inspection and additional operations, paving the way to the possibility for an

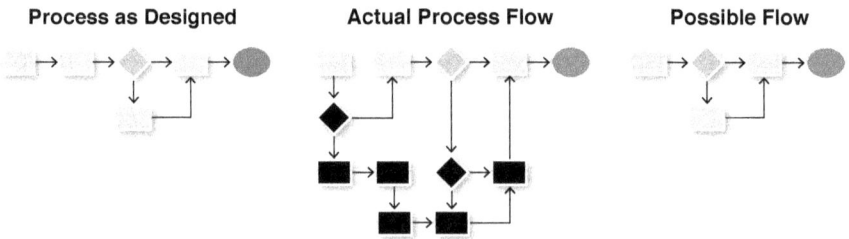

Figure 7 Process as designed, actual process flow, and possible flow.

improved flow. The elimination of black diamonds and black rectangles is achieved through the *prevention* segment of Quality. The improved possible flow results in a cost improvement over the process as designed; it also adds to the capacity of the process, allowing the manufacture of more products utilizing the same resources. This is the improvement segment of Quality. Understanding and acting upon these opportunities can be powerful.

Okay, that was just the manufacturing side of things. What about engineering, supply chain, finance, sales, marketing, human resources…or any other department or activity in your business? The departments in your entire company or any element of your business, be it pharmacy or tire sales, are subject to the same pitfalls as the hidden factory noted above. It all can add cost and/or unnecessary resources, thus impacting negatively the effective operation of your business.

Consider the design process. Is there a structured or gated process for design or process development, or does it just get done? How do you move from concept to production in a timely, cost-effective, competitive timeframe without losing market share or missing an opportunity to eclipse the competition? Does your design team practice DFx (design for: where x = manufacturing, service, repair, safety, test, cost, etc.)? If your product design team is not embracing concurrent design practices with subject matter experts (SMEs) from each of these disciplines, they are potentially adding cost and time to their hidden factory and post manufacturing areas of sales and service, which will also impact other functions within your organization.

There is a big question here. Are you measuring the output performance of any of this? More important, are you measuring the right things, as noted in previous chapters, to drive change? Consider the old axiom, "You can't change what you don't measure."

Takeaway for this chapter: *Inefficient processes and excessive costs due to poor Quality may find their way into the pricing, scheduling, and availability of your product. Compare your processes as designed with how they are actually performing to see whether variation costs are impacting your profitability. When you identify areas of concern and aggressively pursue elimination (prevention) to causes of poor Quality, then move on with (improvement) initiatives that attack and correct process variation and process inefficiencies. You will be implementing solutions that reduce waste and cost and thus positively impact your bottom-line financials.*

9

Keeping Quality on the Radar for Early Warning Alerts

If your company is ISO certified, your compliance segment requires at least an annual review of Quality practices as presented to senior management by the Quality department accountable for compliance to Quality management systems (QMS). Is that really enough to drive change, or does it just report status? Meeting minimum requirements to maintain an industry standard may not be enough to drive the improvement change you seek. Your involvement plays a vital role in assuring that progress continues and Quality behaviors are sustained. Make these reviews work for you by expanding their frequency and holding stakeholders accountable for results, corrective actions, and improvement actions. This is key to achieving sustainable results.

The annual review discusses departmental performance to set Quality objectives as well as results from internal auditors on how departments are performing to standards and internal procedures. Although the ISO minimum requirement is annual, consider the power of a monthly Quality review (or at least quarterly) where departmental performance to Quality metrics and internal audit results are discussed and actioned as necessary. As your Quality department will attest, internal and certification audits deal mostly with assuring that written procedures and required industrial standards other than ISO are complied with. Resolution of previous "findings" will be reviewed for actions and improvement. If, and this is a big *if*, performance metrics are reviewed, the concern is more about demonstration of improvement over time than about the integrity of the metric. Lack of improvement may bring about a notation of "concern" in a certification audit, but not often a notation of "finding," at least by this author's years of experience.

Unfortunately, many companies treat ISO reviews as an administrative necessity. Signoff at the executive level is required, but it's often treated as more of a signatory requirement than as an opportunity for the executive (and staff) to use the process to expand and promote engagement of a cultural approach to Quality.

It's time to make a paradigm shift in behavior. Rather than using the annual ISO requirement for assessment of company performance, move to quarterly reviews (monthly would be even better) to drive a cultural change to Behavior Based Quality (BBQ). Why? This is the best possible place to discuss the status of cascaded corporate objectives (as discussed in earlier chapters). The key to success is twofold. First, top management must schedule and attend the management reviews to show that they are supporting Quality from a cultural CPI perspective. Second, make the management review and actions as positive as possible. Celebrate the successes and action the areas needing improvement with positive support and assured follow-up discussions. The impact of this is profound; no department wants to attend these meetings without having identified, tracked, and set improvement actions to the cascaded company objectives.

Imagine how departmental managers would feel if the reviews were held without senior management represented. The meetings would be nothing more than idle chatter among peers and would have no visible consequences for poor performance nor recognition of success driven from the top. Sure, things might get done and there might be improvement in some areas. But without senior management involvement, how would you know you were addressing the issues of most concern to them? Where do you think the minds of departmental managers would be if senior management were not engaged in the process? It would become nothing more than an exercise; fill the sheet out to be compliant to the management review process. It's important to understand that a good compliance auditor would recognize this and mark the management review process as a "finding," which is considered a non-conformance to the ISO standard.

When management reviews are organized and run by the executive team, a clear message is conveyed to the organization:

We are engaged, we are paying attention, and we expect to see each manager embrace the principle of CPI Quality culture. Although it is important to recognize success, the reviews can be run more efficiently when short honorable mention is given to successes and primary focus is paid to metrics that are missing targets. Specifically, what is being done about corrective action (by the assigned process or metric owner)? What is the prognosis for recovery time to get the metric or objective back on track? These questions must be asked at every management review to assure that proper attention and follow-up is being actioned seriously. These reviews should not take an entire day. Certainly, the size of a company has a bearing on the length of time it takes to conduct a periodic management review; however, when companies use an entire day it's a sign they are not conducting the reviews frequently enough or the focus of the meeting is too broad. A large company that is maintaining compliance with less than ten internal audit findings should be able to conduct the required annual review in less than half a day. This assumes that ongoing performance to objectives and compliance issues are discussed and actioned at least quarterly.

You may not believe that a short meeting can actually cover the necessities required for a management review that meets ISO requirements. Let me assure you, I have actually implemented a process in companies that conduct monthly one- to two-hour reviews. These meetings cover key performance indicators (KPIs) and status to internal audit findings and corrective actions against non-conformances of those findings. These monthly reviews actually have been used with great success as evidence of compliance to their management review requirements with certification agencies. The key, again, is to focus on the corrective action without forgetting to recognize success. In this situation, the discussion might go something like this:

Finance manager: *"There were no non-conformances for the current month in the finance department, and we completed all of our corrective actions from the prior month on schedule with positive results."*

Executive: *"Great job and thanks to the finance team for their efforts. Now let's move on to manufacturing where..."*

This approach provides recognition, but not at the expense of putting focus on the areas that need vetting and thorough discussion about the issue(s), plans, and assignment for corrective actions. In this situation, the discussion may go something like this:

Manufacturing manager: *"Out of the three metrics for manufacturing, the first pass yield for final test met the target of 90% for this month with an expectation of the same for next month. The second metric, for elimination of scrap from $1,500 to $1,000, was not met; the actual for this month was $1,200 in scrap. This was an improvement, but the target was missed due to a missed preventive maintenance operation on the number 3 vertical milling machine that caused machining tolerance issues that could not be reworked. Thus, the material needed to be scrapped. This has been corrected by the facilities manager, who now has this on his night shift maintenance schedule for the end of each month. The third metric...."*

Executive: *"Thanks, Bill, for the report; kudos to your team for their efforts to achieve the FPY target, well done. Regarding the scrap target, it's regrettable, but it appears that you have worked this out. All I would ask at this time is that you work with the facilities manager to assure all machines are on a preventive maintenance schedule...."*

Focus on the business at hand in these review meetings and avoid going off track on discussions that have no relevance or bearing on recognition or corrective actions that bring metrics back to compliance to set company and departmental objectives.

Takeaway for this chapter: *It starts with you as the senior manager/ executive to set the pace of your compliance, prevention, and improvement (CPI) Behavior Based Quality (BBQ) culture and set the requirement for frequent and timely reviews. Change and improvement requires participation from all levels of management to demonstrate commitment to the internal and external strategic Quality objectives in support of a culture of BBQ.*

10

Positioning Quality in the Organization

This chapter is really about where to place the Quality function in your organization. I believe that the best location for Quality is reporting to the top decision maker in a company. Having said that, I will now offer a contradiction. Many variables affect the structuring or restructuring of a company's organization chart. For a variety of reasons, it may not always be possible to structure a company in what I consider the optimal manner. As a company grows, matures, and evolves in its culture, I would always want to point Quality toward reporting to the top decision maker. Table 1 offers some pros and cons to help with your understanding of various Quality reporting structures. I offer this with the intent of helping you make informed decisions when considering where to place Quality in a company's hierarchy.

The challenge for an evolving company is that often there is resistance to change. As your company embarks on a transformational change to a cultural of Behavior Based Quality (BBQ) embracing CPI, there will be resistance to change.

Like safety, Quality performance is based upon behaviors that are intrinsic to and representative of the culture of the company; these should be set and promoted by the top executive and her staff to all employees. If your company has not already established a culture of BBQ, you may experience resistance to cultural change from your staff. If this is the path that you believe will bring success, don't give in.

The benefits will be obvious once results start to be realized. Attaining those results is dependent upon your own behavior of setting the pace of transformation and sticking to it. Here is a bog post that I think has relevance to this discussion:

> *"You can expect the most resistance from those people who have the greatest vested interest in keeping things the same. More often than not, these people are your middle to upper level managers. The reasoning is quite simple; Senior Managers, Directors, and VPs were hired, and are successful at their jobs, because they fit into the organization's current culture. So what is their motivation to change their own behavior?"*
>
> Paula Alsher's Implementation Management Associates (IMA), Inc. Blog posted Sept. 3, 2015.

I think this pretty well sums up what "soft" resistance is all about. I say "soft" resistance because these are not radical demonstrators opposing a philosophical position. They are generally hard workers who are used to things that fit their comfort zone. "This is the way we have always done it." Change is uncomfortable because it is unknown; it's necessary to take the future benefit on faith and trust that the leader is on the right path. Even if you consider your company stable, it may not be functioning well and there may be some form of subtle resistance. Consider: "Oh, sorry Bob. I didn't have time to complete the root cause analysis of why my finance department was two days late to target in closing the books last month." This is where the leader demonstrates his/her commitment to change by not giving in to this behavior, particularly if it is repetitive. One possible response to the finance manager could go like this:

"Well Jim, that is disappointing; I know you want to make the improvements promised. Please set a time for us to get together and discuss your results and corrective actions early next week."

On to structure

No doubt you have been around the block a few times and have seen great variety in how companies are structured. There are two basic formats, functional and matrix. Functional structures are those that have direct reporting lines between each tier level and function in the organization. Matrix organizations are more complex; reporting lines are often blurred across functional structures, where a manager may report to more than one boss. Project organizations typically fall within this format; projects are structured like autonomous organization, yet functions (e.g., Quality) within the project may report to both the project manager and a Quality manager who may have managers reporting to him from multiple other project teams. Companies with multiple regions or global locations and/or those that have multiple product lines are more likely to be structured in a matrix format. There are pros and cons with each structure and there is no "one size fits all" solution. Often the best structure for Quality is what aligns with the size, maturity, culture, product base, location(s), and other variables occurring at that time. I have seen companies restructure several times over a short period, going from functional to matrix and back to functional in order to find the structure that works best. Regardless of type, it remains important to have a central reporting structure where Quality reports at the highest possible level.

Helpful Hint: *When considering organizational structure, it's essential to be flexible and willing to change to meet the needs of the company as it evolves over time.*

This pertains as much to the macro structure of the company as it does to the micro structure at the functional department level. Equally important are reporting relationships. A good reporting relationship between department managers and their management is vital to team accomplishment and employee morale. A poor reporting relationship is likely to be inefficient and perform badly over time. Relationship in this context means having a strong understanding of the function that you are managing. As an example, consider the effectiveness of finance reporting to engineering. Does this sound efficient? Are the agendas of the two organizations the same? One can learn a lot about a company from just looking at its organizational structure and reporting relationships.

One of the first indicators I use to assess a company's Quality culture (or poor commitment to one) is where and to what level of management the Quality function reports. How far away is it from the top executive? The further away the reporting relationship, the more likely it is that Quality initiatives and continuous improvement will be administered sporadically and perhaps with limited focus on the broader organizational functions in the company. This typically means a culture of Quality is not present. More importantly, sustainable financial results and improvement will be harder to achieve over time.

A Quality function reporting to the top level (i.e., president, CEO, COO, owner) has the highest opportunity to successfully set the pace for sustaining CPI BBQ culture that addresses continuous improvement and strives to take non-conformances or any other form of waste to zero. This level of executive support is even more important if you are starting to transform the company culture from control-based to behavior-based. This is where the senior executives set the mission and pace for the transformation that will be driven down into the organization. Stated differently, this is a top-down, not bottom-up, approach to cultural change. I have seen too many instances where a senior executive orders a junior staff member to go out and fix Quality, or dispassionately states that "we need to do something about our Quality." Those lower-level managers and supervisors will do their best to engage workers in improvement, either as a result of the senior-level direction or by their own ambition to make a name for themselves. If the senior executives are not seen by employees at all levels as actively engaged, believing in, and participating in the change process, the transformation to Quality behaviors will not gain the necessary traction for sustainable results.

Setting the reporting position of Quality at the highest level possible is a solid rule of thumb to follow when structuring or restructuring a company. I have worked in or consulted with companies of various sizes ranging from startup to Fortune 100. I strongly believe that Quality must report to the highest level possible in a company, but this may vary based upon size of company, individual expertise, and/or time commitment to the function of Quality if other high-level duties are shared. For example, how effective can a Quality organization be if its "owner" carries a title of vice president of HR and Quality (yes, I have seen this). To be sure, Quality is likely not to get full attention in a growing company where the HR function may take priority over Quality due to staffing needs.

Odd structures like this tend to happen in startup companies or small companies where headcount may be at a financial premium and economics must be considered; after all, as the executive, you are responsible for the profitable viability of the company. Assigning a function to share Quality management can be tough. You want to avoid potential conflict of interest with an assignee who has responsibility for the company's major product output (e.g., manufacturing manager) and Quality. This can work, but it requires a strong ethical manager to keep the lines separated between the shared responsibilities and not get caught up in the push to get product out the door at the expense of Quality. The Quality head must always be ready, able, and willing to say "no" if there is a known Quality escape (non-conformance) in the product.

I once participated in a startup company where in the beginning I managed both operations and Quality. As the company grew, I hired the expertise to manage Quality under me; as the company grew more, that person (because we hired the right set of skills) was promoted to my peer level and became head of Quality. We both reported to the CEO. This highlights the importance of: 1) choosing strong people who can manage multiple functions without compromising the integrity of the company or Quality; and 2) hiring the right talent that is capable of growing within the company as the company grows. Equally important is the ability for management to understand when the company is ready for a change in organizational structure and/or an escalation of the reporting level of Quality. As mentioned above, a default rule of thumb is to always keep Quality reporting as close to the top executive as possible. This will assure visibility, easy access to issues and successes, and showcase the executive' s support and engagement at all levels in Quality.

As mentioned earlier, I once worked with a client who had established a shared responsibility for Quality and HR. When I asked the CEO why Quality reported to the vice president of HR, the CEO responded, "No one else expressed a desire to manage Quality during our startup phase. Bill was also in charge of finance when we were much smaller. When finance became a burden, we hired a CFO and Bill continued to manage HR and Quality." The company was experiencing a surge in growth and the vice president had his hands full trying to fill the staffing resource demand. Quality was not getting the attention it needed and the manager then reporting to the VP was not strong enough to flex with the company. As it turned out, design and manufacturing were both struggling through issues related to Quality. A leader was needed to get them out of the "this is the way we've always done it" syndrome. When we pointed out a few of the manufacturing and design areas needing focus that were not being captured by existing Quality metrics, it became evident to the CEO that they had outgrown the capability of those leading Quality; it was time for an upgrade. This is not to say that those people were doing a bad job or were bad people. They just did not know what they did not know and thus did not look deeper into issues to find true causes rather than symptoms. This experience allowed the CEO to understand that he played a vital role in the development of a Quality culture that was far more than just signing a Quality policy or drafting a mission statement.

Under-hiring or not establishing a clear Quality reporting structure is a common trap that startups and growing companies sometimes fall into. Growing companies with top-down leadership having a focus on Quality culture and continuous improvement seldom struggle through the issue described above.

If you are assuming a functional organization structure rather than a matrix structure, Table 1 may help with some pros and cons of reporting relationships. These are what I consider typical and they may not apply to your company. Your requirements may be unique, so please consider this a guideline for setting up an optimal Quality organization in your company.

This table is intended to give you the pros and cons regarding the various levels where Quality might report in a company's organizational structure. As mentioned earlier, I believe that it's best is always to have Quality report as high as possible in the company's organizational structure, but this is dependent upon a number of variables as we have discussed.

Table 1 Typical functional organization structure relationships.

Typical Title (Level)	Report to: Level / (Title)	Pro	Con
Owner/President/ CEO (Level 0)	Owner/Board of Directors	• Sets the pace and importance of Quality for all employees to easily understand	• **None**, if the Level 0 promotes a culture of Quality behaviors and continuous improvement
Exec. VP/Sr. VP/VP, Quality (Level 1)	**Level 0** (President/CEO)	• Has the attention and the "ear" of the Level 0 so issues can be addressed quickly • Best opportunity to lead and facilitate a cultural change of Quality behaviors as endorsed, supported, and promoted by top executive	• May get mixed message on importance of revenue generation vs Quality
Sr. VP/VP/ Sr. Manager, Quality (Level 2)	**Level 1** (COO/GM)	• Still close to the seat of power and direction • Assuming L1 and L0 are aligned as a team, the messaging and direction should not be compromised	• Greater opportunity for mixed or confusing messaging if COO is not a strong supporter of Quality culture
Sr. VP/VP/Sr. Manager, Quality (Level 2)	**Other Level 1 Technical** (CTO/Exec. VP/ Sr. VP/VP, Engineering)	• Technical support is important for Quality success • Assuming strong Quality behaviors, promotes integration of Quality into design	• Weak Quality behaviors will deteriorate the support and messaging of Quality behaviors, particularly if not driven hard from L0
Sr. VP/VP/Sr. Manager, Quality (Level 2)	**Other Level 1 Non-Technical** (Exec. VP/Sr. VP/VP, Finance, HR, Sales, IT, etc.)	• Still close to seat of power and direction to lead and facilitate the transformation to Quality behaviors • Escalation path is short	• Lack of technical understanding may impact level of support and hinder issue escalation • Non quality department issues may set priorities that impact quality and culture
AVP/Director/Manager, Quality or Quality Assurance (Level 3)	**Level 2 Technical** (Sr. VP/VP/ Sr. Manager, Engineering.)	• Technical support promotes understanding of issues and may promote easier path for issue escalation and corrective action	• Distance from top support makes it more challenging to lead the implementation and maintenance of a Quality culture
AVP/Director/Manager, Quality or Quality Assurance (Level 3)	**Level 2 Non-Technical** (Sr. VP/VP/Sr. Manager, Finance, HR, Sales, IT, etc.)	• Financial and people impact of issues may create better visibility for corrective action	• Distance from top support makes it more challenging to lead the implementation and maintenance of a Quality culture
Sr. Manager/Manager, Quality or Quality Assurance (Level 4)	**Level 3 Technical**	• Understanding of technical Quality issues may be closer to issue cause, thus easier to resolve	• Issue escalation becomes more of a problem • Leading cultural change is much more challenging and likely not sustainable
Sr. Manager/Manager, Quality, Quality Assurance (Level 4)	**Level 3 Non-Technical**	• None from the standpoint of promoting or leading implementation and maintenance of company culture across department boundaries	• Harder to escalate issue through non-technical structure • Positive support to lead cultural Quality transformation is unlikely
Manager/Supervisor/ Lead, Quality, Quality Assurance, Quality Control (Level 5)	**Any Level 4**	• None from the standpoint of promoting or facilitating implementation and maintenance of company culture • May set standards for Quality/ Quality control department	• Too low in the organization to drive impactful, sustainable change across department boundaries

One final thought on structure

People move in and out of positions and companies all the time. New folks who come in at any level may not share the same values of CPI-based Quality behaviors as the predecessor. This is where the reporting structure has the most power. When new employees see and experience the level of executive and management commitment and engagement in building or sustaining a culture of Quality, it should be pretty obvious that their own behavior should mirror that of the company. As one executive explained to a room full of new employees during orientation, "The Quality train is leaving the station; be on it or be left behind." That simple statement said volumes about the direction of the company, leaving no doubt about company commitment to a culture of Quality.

By now you should understand that I believe a company succeeds best when Quality reports to the highest possible level in the company, closest to the top decision maker. The top decision maker sets the pace of the organization and she or he sets the cultural agenda for the entire company. With leadership engagement and commitment to Quality as a business imperative, the transformation to a culture of BBQ has the best chance of success. Success will bring long-term sustainable positive results to the company's bottom-line financials.

Reinforcing Quality behaviors

Let's move on to consider the application of Quality behaviors and performance metrics in departments other than manufacturing where measures are typically focused on quantity versus cause of non-conformances. You might say, why must I measure Quality in finance or any other department in my company? Remember discussion in Chapter 8 on profit from the hidden factory? The message of that chapter is not just for manufacturing. Let's pick on finance for a bit. Although finance is subject to periodic government audits and for ISO certification, internal audits are a necessity, too. But how do you measure Quality other than "audit findings," which are typically symptomatic rather than causal in nature? Because root cause analysis and corrective actions are required responses to audit findings, given that the standards that are set for auditing provide observing a process and its output, doesn't it seem reasonable to set metrics that will indicate cause and frequency of non-compliance to standards?

Waste not, want not

While we are at it, let's also discuss waste as a form of non-conformance that can be measured. For example, let's say that you have set the objective to have the monthly financials closed within the first five days of each month. First, do you measure the days to close books? Second, what do you do with the metric? Is it a graph on the wall, up for all to see? That would be great, but what will you do when the days to close is greater than the target of five days? Closing of financials is a process with many steps that often cross functional boundaries. Thus, the cause of a delay may reside in process steps from other departments such as receiving or purchasing. Are those departments measuring results that show an impact to the closing metric in finance? If these measures are not being tracked, it is likely that you will not see an improvement to the closing metric or a fix to the cause of the delay in finance. The axiom "You can't fix what you don't measure" holds true every time.

Takeaway for this chapter: *Organization structure, reporting relationships, and an understanding of Quality are important for the development and/or maintenance of a compliance, prevention, and improvement (CPI) Behavior Based Quality (BBQ) culture. The closer Quality reports to the top decision maker and chief policy setter, the greater the chance of a successful Quality culture and performance to requirements. Performance to requirements must be measured. Without measures, your team will have no idea about what prevention steps are needed or where improvement opportunity exists. The further Quality is located down in an organization, the more likely issues will not gain the visibility for review and change.*

11

The Role of a
Quality Department

*You can tell a lot about the dynamics of a company by
looking at its organization chart and spending a little time
understanding the reporting relationships and where Quality
is located in the company structure. The role of Quality is
often blurred when it's not fully understood how it should
function in a Behavior Based Quality/compliance, prevention,
and improvement (BBQ/CPI) environment.*

Why should an executive worry about Quality? That's for some lower-level person in the organization to worry about, right? After all, the executive's job is to keep shareholders happy with increasing profits and growth. And therein lies the answer. Poor Quality costs the company money and may impact growth. That money comes directly out of profit and adds to the cost of doing business. Technology, innovation, and "the new best thing" may allow a business to grow and even be successful, but if Quality is poor, the cost of doing things right, after the first time, will erode customer confidence, shrink profits, and eventually impact competitiveness of the product or service and thus the company's growth potential.

I have never run into an executive who wasn't aware of Quality, but their level of understanding and interest ranged from bothersome to "all in" support of why Quality is one of a company's key ingredients to success. If you are not sure why Quality is important, but are interested, please continue with this book; you will learn why you should care about Quality and how "unleashing Quality" can improve your bottom line. If your perception of Quality is close to but not at the "all in" level, then please read on as you will gain additional insight. It will take you to the next level where you understand that Quality can become a competitive advantage to you and your company. If you think that Quality is the responsibility of "the other guy," then definitely look deeper into this book. You will learn why Quality is everyone's job regardless of where you are in the organizational structure of the company or the department in which you work.

I commented earlier in this book that I have seen Quality report to many different levels within a company. Some were at the executive level and some were not. I hope by now you have come to understand that the reporting location has a direct correlation to the Quality culture of the company. The more the executive level is engaged and committed to promoting a compliance, prevention, and improvement (CPI) Behavior Based Quality (BBQ) culture that touches all departments, the easier it is to sustain those cultural behaviors and Quality performance at all levels and functions within the company. In a nutshell, this means that the top person in the company will hire the best person possible to lead Quality by carrying out mandates that set the pace for Quality. Meanwhile, knowing that the Quality direction is in good hands, the top person goes on to lead the other aspects of the business through direct reports of similar high caliber and by imparting her own expertise to profitably grow the company.

Let's go a step further. We established earlier in this book the objective of Quality assurance as CPI. In the last chapter we talked a lot about improving the organizational structure of a company to optimize the impact of Quality by its reporting level. In order to achieve that optimization, we also need to consider the structure of the Quality organization itself. Again, there is no fixed answer to whether a certain format provides the best solution. What you will see below are some guidelines that you can use to establish organizational structure and departmental responsibilities.

Just as the top person in the company sets the pace for the entire organization, the head Quality person: 1) sets the pace that complies with and supports the direction set by the top company official, and 2) sets the pattern of how the Quality organization is structured inclusive of what, where, and how to address CPI. This, of course, assumes you have hired a person who is aligned with your thinking and that you believe that Quality is the cultural mandate to move your company profitably forward.

Start with the basics

Let's start with some basic structural opportunities. What should be the primary functional responsibilities of your Quality organization? Below is a very basic structure that I have found to be a summary of high-level responsibilities. Think of this as a functional design of responsibilities that must be scalable based upon the size of your company and the nature of your product(s), sites, divisional make up, and more. Even a one- or two-person Quality organization or a chef in a restaurant should consider owning, overseeing, or participating in the CPI functions that I have outlined and scale them as appropriate to the company and growth.

If my use of the word *scaling* is unclear, let me explain. In a start-up, one person may be responsible for all Quality CPI functions. The first order of business is to establish guidelines for conformance. As the company grows from product design phase to start of production, it may be necessary for that one person to engage suppliers to assure their level of Quality. This is the start of prevention. When the company grows further and expands the product base and volume, it may be necessary to hire one or more Quality engineers to expand prevention and work in the supplier Quality arenas and perhaps manufacturing processes as well. As the company grows further, and if the right Quality engineers were hired, one of them might be promoted to supplier Quality manager reporting to the original head of Quality. In this sense, the original head of Quality and the hired Quality engineer were scalable, able to expand the responsibilities of their job scope.

Some companies may not need suppler Quality (or other functions of CPI). As an example, supplier Quality may not be necessary in a company providing services that require little or no purchasing support. Supplier Quality has a much greater stake in companies where the primary product is built or integrated from purchased parts and services.

Similarly, in a service organization, supplier Quality may be replaced by a customer satisfaction function that audits and/or obtains feedback from customers on the level of service performance provided to them. In any organization, Quality structure (and its people) must be scalable to the size of the company and the type(s) of products or services that it provides.

Keeping in mind the relationship between Quality and CPI, please consider the following as a guideline for structuring a Quality organization with basic functional responsibilities for each of the three CPI segments.

Compliance: Works cross functionally to document and support internal systems and procedures

- QMS (Quality management systems)
  - Documentation, internal auditing and management reporting
    - □ Manage the repository revision history for company operating procedures
  - Possible source for supplier qualification audits for start-ups and small companies
  - Management reviews
- Inspection
  - Quality control (to the extent necessary)
    - □ Receiving inspection
    - □ In process/final inspection
    - □ Source inspection (to the extent necessary)
- Metrology/calibration
  - Calibration of critical process tooling, jigs/fixtures, measuring equipment, and devices
    - □ All or parts may be outsourced to third-party operators (TPO) but still must be tracked and monitored internally
    - □ Standalone function may only be appropriate for medium to large companies
- Project Quality engineering
  - Product and/or project management proposal support and input for all RFQ, tenders, etc.
    - □ Assesses the Quality requirements of product design for compliance to customer specs and industry standards
    - □ Product Quality staffing, monitoring, and reporting requirements during product lifecycle
    - □ Customer liaison for Quality requirements with internal program management and engineering

- Design review participation to assure conformance to requirements
- Customer deliverable documentation compilation, review and submittal

Prevention: Works cross functionally to facilitate identification of/and conformance to requirements

- Process Quality engineering
  - Design reviews, process review, and/or development
  - Elimination of process non-conformances
- Reliability (if not part of engineering department)
  - Design review, process review
  - Stress testing
  - Failure modes and effects analysis
- Supplier Quality
  - Supplier qualification audits (typically in medium to larger companies)
    - ☐ Requires close working relationship with supply chain/sourcing/purchasing
  - Supplier development and performance assessment
    - ☐ Facilitate supplier process improvement
    - ☐ Implement, monitor, and report supplier performance metrics
- Metrics and assessment
  - Gather and/or consolidate strategic deployment metrics (report as determined)
  - Validation of metric performance (i.e., cost reduction/avoidance) with finance support
- Training
  - Quality awareness training
  - Facilitate strategic deployment process

Improvement: Works cross functionally to facilitate beyond zero non-conformances to eliminate waste and promote Quality in all functional organizations in the company

- Supplier development
  - Take good suppliers to best suppliers*
  - Take best suppliers to best in class*
- Business excellence/operational excellence
  - Internal organizational function (preferably under Quality) that facilitates establishes new processes or improves existing processes that have achieved a zero-non-conformance rating
- Quality culture training
  - Extends Quality awareness into cultural behavior training
- Facilitating process development, mapping, and improvement
  - Establishing process steps and requirements

Note: Don't lose sight of the fact that best suppliers can always be better. Sometimes best implies that no work must be done to maintain or improve by being better at what they do.

Does a hybrid approach work?

You have probably figured out by now that I am biased toward Quality as a singular organization reporting to the highest possible level of company authority and leadership. Having said that, what about what I call *hybrid structures*? This is where Quality and another function are combined—such as Quality and HSE (health, safety, and environment), or security, or reliability and testing—where Quality is the lead organization. This is a bit different from what I discussed earlier, where Quality was under another organization. In this hybrid approach, Quality is noted as the lead function. This actually is fairly common in many industries and it can work from a Quality perspective. The same concerns of exposure and focus are present for the secondary organization as they were in earlier examples when Quality was a secondary functional responsibility.

With that in mind, let's press this issue a little further to see whether we can make this work. Let's use a structure of Quality and HSE as an example. I always worry about the level of support given to the second function mentioned (HSE for this example). Is that function being supported properly? Does the head of Quality and HSE have the intellectual background to support both functions alone to the benefit of the company? Where I have found this structure to be most successful is when the head of Quality and HSE has a subject matter expert manager leading each of the functions and reporting to him or her. When properly staffed, this can work; however, I believe this hybrid type of structure is best suited for start-ups or small companies that are not yet large enough to scale these functions to independent organizational entities. The key message here is to hire (and pay) above your need so the person can become an integral part of growing your company rather than an observer.

Time for a short side note on HSE. One of the reasons I can be positive about this particular pairing of functions is that Quality and HSE are very much alike. They are both behaviorally based and their performance is set by the culture of the company. To this point, I believe and strongly support that HSE needs (ultimately) to report as high in the organization as Quality.

It is all about the pairing

I mentioned previously that security and reliability work as possible participants in a hybrid organization structure. I believe that security (as in facility security, guard station, surveillance) is more a function of facilities organization; these departments work best reporting to that function or as a peer to that function or under the largest "occupier" of facility real estate, such as manufacturing/operations.

Reliability, on the other hand, is an interesting point to ponder; by its very nature it is focused on Quality—Quality of design and functionality for the product's intended use as well as the processes used in the manufacturing of the product. In this case poor process Quality could limit the reliability of the product, thus leading to premature failure even if the design is robust in nature. Most companies tend to place the reliability function within an engineering organization because the analysis of failure mechanisms and stress analysis tend to be an integral part of the engineering technical function. Some might argue for a check and balance approach and separate these two functions, but I believe that engineering is the best location for the reliability function. Having said that, let me also say that if the reliability function in your company is more of a surveillance function dealing with calculating product information and customer feedback into mean time between failure (MTBF) or mean time to repair (MTTR), then Quality could be an acceptable home.

Note: *A rule of thumb would be to structure behavior-based functions together (e.g., Quality and safety) and align functional organizations along logical lines of technical expertise (e.g., engineering and reliability) or similar functions or similar interfaces such as sales and marketing.*

The focus of this chapter has been to address some basic functional responsibilities within a Quality department. The next step would be to define opportunities for various organizations in a company to improve Quality through measurement. For some simple metrics that can be used to drive change in various organizations within a company, please refer to Chapter 12 for samples of departmental metrics.

Takeaway for this chapter: *As noted in previous chapters, there is no "one size fits all" structure for Quality. The structure of Quality organization depends upon the size of a company, its culture, product types, processes involved, and much more. However, in a compliance, prevention, and improvement (CPI) based culture of Quality, the example functions for Quality noted in this chapter define roles that fit best in each of the three tenets of CPI. This should provide some guidelines for organizational structure of Quality and functions of a CPI-based Quality organization that supports and facilitates the cultural direction of the company's executives.*

12

Guidance on Metrics that Drive Change

As part of CPI (compliance, prevention, and improvement) behaviors, metrics must be established that drive change and support the cascaded top-level company objectives. This chapter provides examples of metrics that can be used for prevention and improvement in numerous departments. Compliance behaviors are achieved by establishing, maintaining, and reviewing these metrics and by auditing for conformance to established and documented processes and procedures.

This chapter provides simple recommendations for departmental metrics that can support cascaded objectives and drive improvement. At the very least, they should be representative of basic departmental performance.

It is very important to understand that effect-type metrics must be supported by lower-level cause-type metrics in order to be able to make a change from X to Y by a certain date. Without this information, you will not know what issue is causing the poor performance that must be improved. Typically, cause-type metrics define the barriers to success, thus providing insight as to what must be improved in order to achieve the stated goal.

Note: *The following metric examples all follow the same format: department name followed by an indented effect-type metric, followed by an indented target to improve (TTI).*

Accounting
- A/P cycle time
  - Reduce cycle time from X to Y by [date]
- A/P errors
  - Decrease A/P errors from X to Y by [date]

Engineering
- Design errors (caught in design review)
  - Improve design review performance from X to Y by [date]
- Concept to market cycle time (time to market—TTM)
  - Decrease TTM from X to Y by [date]

Finance
- Days to close monthly financial books
  - Improve book closing from X days to Y days by [date]
- Journal entry errors
  - Decrease journal errors from X to Y by [date]
- Time to profitability (TTP)[1]
  - Decrease TTP from X to Y by [date]

Human resources
- Retention date
  - Improve employee retention from X% to Y% by [date]
- Requisition to hire cycle time
  - Decrease hire cycle time from X to Y by [date]

Manufacturing/operations
- On-time delivery performance (OTD)
  - Improve OTD from X to Y by [date]
- In-process inspection reject/yield rate[2]
  - Decrease rejects from X to Y by [date]
- Final inspection first pass yield (FPY)[2]
  - Improve FPY from X to Y by [date]
- Equipment/machine availability (up time)[3]
  - Improve availability from X to Y by [date]

Marketing
- Customer satisfaction index (CSI)
  - Improve CSI from X to Y by [date]
- Market penetration
  - Move from X% penetration to Y% of market by [date]
- Marketing campaign ROI
  - Improve campaign ROI from X to Y by [date]

Material management/inventory control
- Inventory turns
  - Increase inventory turns from X to Y by [date]
- Excess & obsolete inventory (E&O)
  - Decrease E&O dollars from X to Y by [date]
- Cycle count accuracy
  - Improve cycle count of A level parts from X to Y by [date]
  - Improve cycle count of B level parts from X to Y by [date]
  - Improve cycle count of C level parts from X to Y by [date]
- Kit shortages
  - Improve kitting shortages from X to Y by [date]

Reliability
- Mean time to failure (MTTF)[4]
  - Improve MTTF from X to Y by [date]
- Mean time between failure (MTBF)[4]
  - Increase MTBF from X to Y by [date]

Sales
- Sales forecast accuracy
  - Improve sales forecast accuracy from X to Y by [date][5]

Service
- Service response time
  - Improve service response from X to Y by [date]
- Equipment/product availability (field up time)[6]
  - Improve service availability from X to Y by [date]
- Mean time to repair (MTTR)[7]
  - Improve MTTR from X to Y by [date]

Supply chain

- MRP accuracy to demand
  - Improve MRP accuracy from X to Y by [date]
- Buys required inside part lead-time
  - Reduce inside lead time buys from X to Y by [date]

Notes by the number:

1) TTP is a measure that can be impacted by cost, price, OTD, time to market, design integrity, and more; be sure to identify causes in order to seek the proper corrective action to focus on the right area for improvement.

2) FPY, reject rate, and pass rate are similar measures that typically address first occurrence. You should also be measuring second- and third-pass yield numbers if rejects continue; this signifies a deeper issue if rejects continue after initial rework. Inspection metrics can be misleading if causes are not identified. The only way that true corrective action can occur is to prevent the causes of errors.

3) Up time is a better measure than down time, because machine scheduling in MRP or factory scheduling systems is based upon availability.

4) MTTF and MTBR metrics typically should be used as feedback to design engineering and/or manufacturing process (based on cause) owners for corrective actions.

5) Sales forecast accuracy has a direct impact on factory scheduling and thus MRP accuracy, part shortages, buys inside lead-time and OTD. Having an integrated sales and operations planning session on a regular basis can improve this.

6) Field up time is usually needed for mission-critical equipment where equipment operation is imperative to customer success (e.g., network servers, phone systems, power generation equipment).

7) MTTR is an important measure for service organizations and should be used as feedback to design engineering. Product design should incorporate service/repair ease into their designs.

Takeaway for this chapter: *These are general examples of departmental metrics to use as guidelines for the individual and specific needs of your company. The key is the use of SMART metrics that identify the pulse of the company and its direction. Frequent reviews of these metrics while holding stakeholders accountable can provide early warning indicators of success or movement in the wrong direction. Don't be mislead or caught up with what often is referred to as "best practice." This implies that there is no need to improve. I prefer the phrase "better practice" as it leaves room for improvement.*

13

Getting Your BBQ Working

Behavior can be defined as a set of repeatable actions that become acceptable and commonplace. Changing behaviors at work requires actions set by a desire to change and improve. This simple approach is more about encouraging you and the management team to think differently about Quality so as to properly engage the entire company in adopting new thinking about behaviors that support compliance, prevention, and improvement (CPI) based Quality. Cultural transformation is easiest when led from the top. Sometimes, however, the need for change is recognized lower in the organization. This chapter will give you an idea of what a Behavior Based Quality (BBQ) culture looks like in a company and then lead you through a process of how to get there if it doesn't exist.

Throughout this book you have read the words Behavior Based Quality (BBQ). I wanted to set the basics of Quality up front with reference to BBQ as the end game. Focusing on BBQ earlier may have dissuaded you from the core message regarding the importance of a strategy for a culture of Quality that includes organizational accountability and structure and adoption of CPI behaviors. Now that we have that out of the way, more discussion of BBQ is in order. Specifically, why is it important and how do we implement a company culture focused upon certain behaviors?

You have likely heard the phrases "work safe," "be safe," and "think safety." Thinking and acting are behaviors. Today, in more and more industries, you will see the acronym SBC—safety-based culture. It is this culture of safety that has brought about profound reduction in a total recordable incident rate (TRIR) for many companies. We think of safety as related to dangerous and perhaps even deadly events when not practiced properly, so clearly it gets our attention. Why don't we think of Quality in this same manner? In a behavior-based culture of safety, every employee in every department has an involvement and accountability to practice safety behaviors.

Traditionally when people think of Quality the words that come to mind are *control* and *assurance*. These are not behaviors. Control is typically a reaction to post-event issues and assurance attempts to address pre-events by making sure Quality practices, policies, and procedures are in place and followed. The problem is that both approaches provide little to no organizational structure for sustainable performance improvement or cultural change that would embrace Quality as a behavioral necessity.

In support of this behavioral approach, please consider the three tenets of BBQ—compliance, prevention, and improvement (CPI). These are the foundation of Quality behaviors. Quality doesn't just happen. One needs to take the initiative (in priority order) to comply with requirements, prevent errors, and improve processes. These are behaviors that drive a culture of BBQ.

Let me be more clear

BBQ is not QMS, it is bigger than that. When a culture of BBQ exists, it is promoted and led from the top and cascaded down into the organization so that every employee participates equally in compliance (conformance to requirements), prevention (of non-conformances), and improvement (of processes to reduce all forms of waste). It's possible to have bits of these in different parts of the company, but if not led, promoted, and supported from the top, BBQ will not be sustainable; the rush for revenue and profit may be met, but will become a constant "firefight."

Let's explore more deeply the Quality tenets that comprise a BBQ culture. The three legs of our BBQ provide stability in all situations. CPI are the foundational elements of our BBQ and necessary to achieve sustainable results.

Compliance: Conformance to requirements…all requirements!

Prevention: Relentlessly seek to understand the cause of errors and mistakes and use the tools of Quality to prevent them from recurring by assuring conformance to requirements.

Improvement: *After* prevention is implemented, use the plethora of improvement tools available to create change that eliminates waste of all types.

When you get right down to it, this is pretty simple and straight-forward; there's nothing terribly complex or confusing about the intent. It is the "doing" that creates the challenge.

What does a BBQ culture look like?

When a culture of BBQ exists, it is promoted and led from the top. That's easy to say, because most Quality policies are issued or at least signed by the top executive. In practice, a Quality policy or even a mission statement does not create or sustain a culture. The behaviors of the top executive and management team are what starts the drum beat of the organization. That drum beat sets the pace for requirements that flow down into the organization. A few annual objectives set at the top and cascaded down to develop a roll-up contribution from each department against the three BBQ tenets (compliance, prevention, and improvement) will identify cost performance around Quality behaviors that contribute to the company's bottom-line results. With continued reinforcement from the top, sustainable results will continue and a culture of Quality will be like breathing; it just comes naturally.

Here are a few simple examples of a culture of BBQ

- Every department has a set of monetized metrics against each of the CPI elements.

- Process owners accept accountability for CPI performance.

- Metrics are used as positive reinforcement for change.

- Anyone can stop a product/process/service delivery for Quality cause with no recrimination.

- Your customers recognize and support the efforts that you are putting into cultural change for Quality.
- Continued learning of improvement tools and methods is taking place.
- Suppliers are asking for help with their Quality programs.
- Executives take time to recognize CPI behaviors and team contributions.

For years we have been led to believe that Quality is about *assuring* that Quality functions are in place and *controlling* process output through inspection and cost reduction initiatives. These traditional approaches have channeled our thinking and actions to focus primarily on manufacturing and service functions. Naturally, we believe that this is where the largest impact to our profits occur; these have become the largest opportunity areas for cost avoidance and cost reduction. It's not too far off the mark, but what about where manufacturing output starts, back in the bid and proposal stages prior to design of product or service? What about design (e.g., engineering or menu planning), product/service costing, financial control, product/program management, marketing, and sales? If you are not getting Quality correct from the beginning and maintaining it in all areas of your company, you are leaving behind unrealized opportunity cost and profit that will fail to optimize your bottom-line financial performance. Equally important is that these departments will fail to learn the Quality contribution that they can make to the success of the company.

How do you know if the BBQ is working?

By now I hope you understand that compliance, prevention, and improvement are the tenets of Quality that constitute the culture of BBQ promoted and supported by the top executive of the company. When this company has a strategy of short- and long-term objectives and these have been established and cascaded down into the organization for all employees, then I believe it is safe to say your BBQ is working.

What if you don't have a BBQ?

The challenge of understanding how behaviors relate to Quality is that this is not the way people typically think (about Quality) in a work environment. It is much easier to relate behaviors to safety than Quality. Let's take a simpler approach to thinking about Quality. We think about Quality of life and the Quality of our food, drinking water, air, service, entertainment, and just about every aspect that directly affects us. Moreover, we tend to be willing to take actions to improve poor Quality in our non-work environment. These actions set behaviors.

Most Quality books or articles tend to focus on the tools of Quality and how to use the many variations Lean Six Sigma and/or other well-known tools to bring about waste reduction and cost savings. These are just tools. By themselves they do not create Quality nor sustain Quality. They need a unifying force to align their functions and create sustainable value. *People's behaviors can be that unifying force needed to bring sustainable, value-driven results to Quality.*

When using Quality tools, the question to ask is whether Quality is really improving. Incremental savings may be achieved, but have they improved Quality to a level of sustainability? Inconsistent use or misapplication of Quality tools often brings about a false sense of accomplishment. The reality is that you may be making bad parts faster and cheaper by focusing on *improvement* and not adding *compliance* and *prevention* to the action plan first. Thus, the cost of poor Quality (COPQ) may not have been improved at all.

This is compounded when Quality is thought of primarily as an add-on to manufacturing or service-related functions with little consideration given to the "softer" organizational departments of HR, sales, marketing, finance, accounting, and others. When observing companies with this type of operational dynamic, it's easy to see that a culture of Quality is not overtly present. The behaviors that are needed to drive a culture of Quality are in desperate need of stimulation, enhancement, nurturing, and growth. In these situations, there are great hidden treasures of bottom-line financial opportunities left untapped in all of the other functional departments of the company. Quality applies to every department and every employee is accountable for Quality in a BBQ culture.

Sadly, most books and articles don't address Quality behaviors or how to achieve a sustainable culture of Quality. Historically there has always been a focus on the money generators through Quality control and Quality assurance of manufacturing and service functions; these have led us to think that this is where Quality belongs. Even as companies have evolved into a greater Quality awareness, the control and assurance mindset continues as the hallmark of today's approach to Quality, augmented by, and sometimes confused with, the integration of Lean Six Sigma.

The attempt to achieve sustainable results has been fed by constant fretting over metrics through management engagement ranging from brow beating to ambivalence. Less enlightened companies frequently fall (or continue to fall) into allowing bottom-line financial results to be the primary driving pressure. Once pressure is released, things fall back into their previous levels of performance.

Have you ever wondered why Quality keeps coming up as a topic of discussion in senior staff meetings and in the boardroom? Stuff happens, right? It would only be natural that the topic of Quality comes up when things have slipped through the cracks and problems occur. But we have a Quality department, you say. Why are they not fixing this? Why are they allowing this to happen? Why can't they stop it? We have put fixes in place for past non-conformance; why are problems recurring? Based upon the frequency and severity of issues that arise, it's likely that you have not implemented sustainable CPI-based solutions. It's an indicator that BBQ is not working.

Survival of the fittest and achieving sustainable results

Let's get real; business is about survival of the fittest in a highly competitive world. Sustainable solutions are necessary for a successful business and financial results will likely always be the final measure of success. The challenge for a cultural shift is to marry Quality behaviors with the need to accomplish financial measures of success. Here are a few thoughts on that topic.

First, in order to achieve sustainable results, it's essential to embrace Quality as a cultural and business imperative. This requires commitment, dedication, and patience along with support from the top executive who cascades requirements down into the organization to every department. This book deals with the role of executives in this transformation; if you have not yet reached that point in your career and you are a lower-level manager, consider the three-step process to follow in this chapter.

Second, assess the existence or health of the culture of Quality in your company. If your solution to issues is reactionary, with actions that drive for a quick fix then move on, you do not have a culture of sustainable Quality behaviors. Tough words, but it's important to understand what the behaviors are that will drive and sustain a culture of Quality. Below we will look at what a BBQ culture looks like and explore some tips on how to bring about sustainable long-term results.

Third, does your company have a strategy for Quality? It's more than just an organization named Quality; it's an actual plan to implement, improve, and sustain Quality practices and behaviors throughout your organization. In smaller companies, this must be more than just a slogan on the wall. It must be methodically planned and implemented as a cultural imperative. For larger companies, the establishment of an organizational structure supporting a BBQ culture can bring about profound positive results to your financial bottom line when practiced and supported from the top executive down to the employee level in each department. While company leaders promote and support the cultural shift, members of the Quality department may be well suited to facilitate training that accompanies and supports the cultural transformation.

I'm a Quality professional and believe in BBQ. What do I do?

If you are not an executive yet, but are on the path to building your career and you believe in BBQ, what do you do in a situation where Quality isn't being driven as a cultural imperative from the top? Cultural change is not impossible, but it takes time, patience, and courage to convince management that BBQ works. As managers, you and your peers may be the key to getting the cultural change started. Consider the following three-step process as a possible path to building a convincing argument supporting the necessity and value of BBQ.

Step 1 – Start with your own department.
- Adopt and learn the philosophy of CPI behaviors.
  - Train your staff in the elements of CPI.
  - Determine which tools will work best, based on employee skill levels.
- Use SMART metrics to define and prioritize areas to improve.
  - Establish "dollarized" metrics for each of the CPI tenets for each department that you manage.
  - Set baseline measures of performance.
  - Set accountability for your department heads, leads, and employees.
  - Measure and document change over time.

Always use SQDC (safety, Quality, delivery, cost) as the basis to set priorities. When safety and Quality are set in that order, delivery and cost will follow accordingly. We have all seen what happens when delivery or cost is put in front of safety or Quality.

Step 2 – Evangelize your department's results of positive change.
- Demonstrate success and improvement opportunities to other department heads.
  - Stress CPI as the philosophy and SQDC as the prioritization mechanism.
- Train other department heads in CPI.
  - Give department heads the guidelines from step 1.
- As training is accepted, assist with metric development.
  - Identify low-hanging fruit to change.
- Provide training in tool use.
- Track changes over time, evangelize improvement.
  - Win over new devotees.
- Report results to management.

Continue to promote SQDC as the basis for setting priorities.

Step 3 – Gain management engagement.
- Using results from steps 1 and 2, solicit management to expand CPI in select departments.
  - Pick low-hanging fruit areas (engineering, finance, HR, process stuff); follow steps 1 and 2.

- Implement at least quarterly management reviews of CPI metrics.
  - Use this forum to market and demonstrate results of CPI metrics.
  - Recognize results and hold process owners accountable.
  - Use reviews as positive reinforcement for the value proposition of change.
  - *This is where management recognizes Quality as a cultural imperative and a desirable behavior.*
- Gain management support to incorporate CPI in all remaining departments.
  - Use management reviews to recognize success and understand cause of failures.
  - Hold teams accountable to achieve sustainable results through CPI behaviors.
- Get top management to tie next year's objectives to CPI metrics.

Are there any further suggestions to help achieve success?

It goes without saying that sustainable results and cultural change cannot be achieved (or at best will be short lived) if management is not engaged as a believer and participant in BBQ's cultural ability to make a solid contribution to the company's bottom-line financial results. Top management must set clear company performance objectives and cascade those objectives down into the organization. Every department must be tasked to define and contribute to its part of those objectives. On a monthly basis, determine results by department and then "roll up" results to summarize the company's top-level performance to the cascaded objectives. In this manner, Quality performance is tied to company financial performance for all departments. CPI performance metrics are always monetized to properly show the impact in dollar contribution to the bottom line. Most importantly, every department makes a contribution, whether in direct cost reduction or indirect reduction in overhead and SG&A costs and expenses. Through monthly management reviews, everyone holds everyone accountable to do their part. Department managers are supportive in the use, training, and sharing of Quality tools with other departments and do not rely on others to do the work for them. Top management sets timely performance reviews and participates by acknowledging issues (positively), requiring follow-up to assure issues are addressed, and participates in and/or leads in recognizing successes.

Takeaway for this chapter: *Have no illusions, cultural transformation is not for the faint of heart. It will be challenging and you may meet resistance from many levels. This type of change in an established company is not implemented by decree nor left to lower-level managers to create and implement. Although cultural change to Behavior Based Quality (BBQ) may have its initial roots in the Quality organization, successful implementations must eventually be led from the top as a cultural imperative to business success. It takes time and willingness for people to understand that this is a business necessity and that it establishes what modern Quality is about. Use your successes to prove the value of BBQ and you will be rewarded with a cultural evolution that achieves sustainable results through the proper use of Quality tools that are aligned with compliance, prevention, and improvement. Remember, a sustainable culture of BBQ is like breathing; it just happens.*

14

Notes & Conclusion

There always seems to be a bit more that I want to say, so this section of the book has some final comments related to things that matter to me when it comes to a culture of Quality. Now that you have read this book, I hope that you have come to realize the importance of Quality, why it matters, and, most importantly, how it can bring results to your financial bottom line once you have chosen to promote and support a Behavior Based Quality (BBQ) culture as the company's leader.

What if you are not a manufacturer or large company?

As I said much earlier in this book, it shouldn't matter, but it was just plain easier to write this book in the context of a company providing manufactured products or services. This is where American culture has failed to sustain its leadership. I think small companies or individual proprietors of service or product "get it," but big corporations still fall prey to the profit motive of here and now, this quarter, this year or bust. Our friends in the orient seem to take a longer view of things and are less financially quarter driven and more driven by the SQDC model (safety, Quality, delivery, cost) that is generally measured more stringently than profit. The belief here is that if you have sustainable safety and Quality behaviors in place, delivery (on time) and cost (improvement) will follow naturally. If you put either cost or delivery in front of safety or Quality as a priority, you will fail. A recent example of this is the German manufacturer of diesel automobiles that forsook safety and Quality for delivery. Billions of dollars later in penalties, fines, buybacks and rebates and of course customer satisfaction, they may be thinking differently about SQDC. So please don't be upset with me for describing things in a manufacturing or service manner that may be more recognizable to corporate readers. The message, in my humble opinion, is easily translated to any business regardless of size. It's all about scaling and setting a mindset of Behavior Based Quality (BBQ).

People matter

Let's dwell a bit more on people for a moment; in particular, well tenured individuals in key leadership or positions where they hold a position of subject matter expertise (SME). Age may or may not be a factor, but some people refer to them (regardless of age or gender) as graybeards.

This may not be a very politically correct term to use; in some industries, it actually is a term of endearment and respect for knowledge and capability. As you might guess from the term, the reference is to senior individuals who have gained respect and accolades for their SME, breadth of knowledge, and possible longevity in their field. While senior management in a company may set the strategy for market direction, more often than not, it is these well-experienced people who critique and hone that strategy into a viable product, service, or process.

Unfortunately, in many companies, these SMEs may be the unsung heroes with little recognition for years of faithful service and positive work ethic that is the essence of the generation in which they were raised. When supported, their sage advice is the hallmark of mentoring and growing junior or less experienced staff.

These people may be in senior management roles, but managing a staff dilutes their SME contribution; thus, we often find them positioned as individual contributors who are out of the everyday requirements of managing other than providing guidance and mentoring. Recognition can be as simple as titling them: chief technical officer, fellow, senior advisor, or other term related to their area of expertise. Basically, whatever fits the culture of your company, assuming your company recognizes subject matter expertise.

These well-experienced people are a valuable resource. They can function as members of industry affiliations and consortiums to set standards, promote the company in events, and mentor younger individuals to achieve stature by setting the expectation for learning, work ethics, and collaboration with internal and external sources of knowledge that support the growth of a company. SMEs are some of the best representatives to set the technical requirements for Quality practices as well as product and industry standards.

Case Study

A client company had in its employ a tenured senior manager of Quality tasked with reducing operating costs and improving Quality. The manager had visited each department in the company from finance to engineering. In his rounds of discussions he had facilitated the discovery of opportunities to reduce net annualized costs. This process led to identification of nearly 70 improvement projects totaling an annualized amount of $50 million across the broad range of departments and functions. Of course, all projects could not be acted upon at the same time. There simply were not enough resources to accomplish them all at once, so they were spread out over the year with project owners, all facilitated by the senior manager. After about four months, improvement projects were running along smoothly and nearly 20% of the reduction opportunities had been realized and documented by finance as actual contribution to improved gross margin. Unfortunately, the industry was going through a downturn, and the company needed to take some very tough and quick actions to sustain profit margins against a declining sales base. Management quickly called for a reduction in force (RIF). The senior manager, not having a staff and being an individual contributor, was one of the employees impacted by the RIF. He was well compensated and had no staff that would be impacted by his absence, so it seemed logical that his salary loss (along with others) would contribute the necessary dollars to maintaining profit. Without a facilitator to guide, assist, and mentor project owners with improving processes and reducing costs, the projects ceased to be a priority. Thus, the opportunity for $50 million in verified savings was never realized.

The lesson to consider in this case study is to think beyond the quick and easy response. There may be more cost reduction potential than the salary of one or more well experienced persons. A possible solution would be to pool your graybeards and well experienced individuals and assign them the task of identifying "X" times their salary in verifiable cost savings or other improvements amounting to more than the value of their dismissal. Like SMART metrics, discussed earlier, this approach can be time based, thus providing incentive as well as possible time for market conditions to turnaround. More often than not, this will allow a company to come out of the downturn in better condition than when it went in. This takes bravery on the part of management because it is contrary to typical management behavior and what is believed to be tried and true actions.

Managers versus leaders

Another people matter has to do with the distinction between managers and leaders. Can a person be both? In my opinion, lots of people become managers of people, but that does not mean they are leaders of people. *Managing* is the manner in which we do our daily tasks and assignments. Those tasks and assignments may include telling other people what to do and when. *Leadership* is how we inspire our team (those we are tasked to manage) to achieve levels of performance and personal excellence that were not thought achievable by supporting, mentoring, and demonstrating that all things are possible when we, as individuals or members of a team, put our minds and hearts to work to accomplish the challenges set for us. This forms the basis of learning and growing an organization that develops its people so that they may rise to new positions based on their capabilities during the course of their career. So, in my opinion, leaders may be managers, but managers are not always leaders. Certainly some people can be both.

Transformational change

My background spans a number of industries and a broad spectrum of positions from engineer to executive, and some of my most significant learnings have come to me while managing Quality, albeit later in my career. Quality is the function that helped bring all my many disparate learnings together for me. Consider me an evangelist who wants to teach executives and aspiring managers that there is a place for Quality in any functional department in a company. Moreover, it is the cultural change of behaviors that transforms thinking to bring success to companies. My goal is to help those interested in a better way to achieve success for themselves and the companies for which they work. I hope this book has inspired you to think and behave differently about Quality.

In conclusion

Writing this book has been a passion of mine for a number of years. I have been blessed to work for a number of great companies, most recently one led by a CEO who had the courage and fortitude to know what he didn't know about Quality. He came to the realization that Quality could become a market differentiator if properly integrated into the DNA and culture of the company. Although Quality is not what I would consider my career "native language," from an educational standpoint I have always been what I choose to call an evangelist of change. Participating in the cultural change process brought about my final conversion to BBQ as a vital and important factor to a company's success. Writing this book has allowed me to coalesce my thoughts, observations, and experiences from various industries and work experiences throughout my career. The consultancy that I have set up to *unleash Quality* is an act of passion to help executives understand the importance of a BBQ culture and how it can bring about positive change when centered on compliance, prevention, and improvement.

Appendix A
The Gurus of Quality

I couldn't write this book without paying homage to those I consider to be the primary gurus of Quality. These four set the foundation for the evolution of modern Quality. Since their passing and well into the future, I am confident that Quality will continue to evolve in ways beyond any expectations.

Here is a brief biographical summary of these Quality icons taken from Wikipedia.

Please note that Wiki is an open architecture on-line reference source that may be subject to on-going updates or changes. My intention was to capture the essence of the background and the contributions made by these four Quality gurus. Should you have greater interest in any or all of these individuals, you will easily find sources that provide more timely and/or accurate information. This Wiki material should be read as informational, but may be subject to interpretation or on-line edits or changes.

Joseph Juran (December 24, 1904 – February 28, 2008)

Juran is widely credited for adding the human dimension to the concept of Quality management. He pushed for the education and training of managers. Juran believed it was essential to isolate human relations problems and he also believed that resistance to change was the root cause of Quality issues. Juran's concept of Quality management extended outside the walls of the factory to encompass nonmanufacturing processes, especially those that might be thought of as service related.

Juran was one of the first to write about the cost of poor Quality. This was illustrated by his "Juran trilogy," an approach to cross-functional management composed of three managerial processes: Quality planning, Quality control, and Quality improvement. Without change, there will be a constant waste; during change, there will be increased costs; after improvement, margins will be higher and the increased costs will be recouped.

Juran (who focused on managing for Quality) went to Japan in 1954 and started teaching courses in Quality management for top and middle management. The idea that top and middle management needed training had been met with resistance in the United States. In Japan, it would take some 20 years for the training to pay off; by the 1970s, Japanese products began to be seen as the leaders in Quality. This sparked a crisis in the United States due to Quality issues in the 1980s.

W. Edwards Deming (October 14, 1900 – December 20, 1993)

Deming is best known for his work in Japan after WWII, where he made a significant contribution to Japan's later reputation for innovative, high-Quality products, and for its economic power. He is regarded as having had more impact upon Japanese manufacturing and business than any other individual not of Japanese heritage. Despite being honored in Japan in 1951 with the establishment of the Deming prize, he was only just beginning to win widespread recognition in the United States at the time of his death in 1993. President Reagan awarded him the National Medal of Technology in 1987. The following year, Deming also received the Distinguished Career in Science award from the National Academy of Sciences.

Deming is also known for a system of thought he called the System of Profound Knowledge, consisting of four components, or "lenses," through which to view the world simultaneously:

- Appreciation of a system
- Understanding of variation
- Psychology
- Epistemology, or a theory of knowledge

Philip Crosby (June 18, 1926 – August 18, 2001)

Crosby initiated the Zero Defects program at the Martin Company and went on to grow his career as a Quality professional in large corporations in the United States. In 1979, Crosby started the management consulting company Philip Crosby Associates, Inc. This consulting group provided educational courses in Quality management both at their headquarters in Winter Park, Florida, and at eight foreign locations. Also in 1979, Crosby published his first business book, *Quality Is Free.* This book would become popular at the time because of the crisis in North American Quality. During the late 1970s and into the 1980s, North American manufacturers were losing market share to Japanese products largely due to the superior Quality of the Japanese goods.

Crosby's response to the Quality crisis was the principle of "doing it right the first time" (DIRFT). He included four major principles:

1. The definition of Quality is conformance to requirements (requirements meaning both product and customer requirements).

2. The system of Quality is prevention.

3. The performance standard is zero defects (relative to requirements).

4. The measurement of Quality is the price of non-conformance.

He believed that an organization that established a Quality program would see savings that more than pay off the cost of the program: "Quality is free."

Philip Crosby's legacy continues in the consulting company he founded, Philip Crosby & Associates, with the addition of a fifth principle: *The purpose of Quality is to create customer success.* The five principles remain the basis of the company's consulting practice.

Kaoru Ishikawa (July 13, 1915 – April 16, 1989)

Ishikawa was a Japanese organizational theorist and professor on the faculty of engineering at the University of Tokyo, noted for his Quality management innovations. He is considered a key figure in the development of Quality initiatives in Japan, particularly the Quality circle. He is best known outside Japan for the Ishikawa or cause-and-effect diagram (also known as fishbone diagram) often used in the analysis of industrial processes. This process of analysis involved the review of possible causes related to people, material, environment, equipment, process, and management. These form the basic areas for the assessment of the possible causes that effect the occurrences of non-conformances.

Appendix B
Workbook Checklist

Many tests and surveys can be found and used to rate the effectiveness of a Quality department and the awareness of or commitment to Quality in a company. Many of the questions in these surveys give insight as to the culture of a company as it relates to Quality. Simple awareness of Quality is not an indication of a culture of Quality, because culture is more about behaviors when no one is looking. Behavior Based Quality (BBQ) as described in this book is like breathing; it just happens.

When I take on a new client, I try to keep initial meetings simple and high level. If the results bring the executives to action with only a few hours of their time, then value has been added and we can move on to more specific discussions and proposals for action and improvement.

In these initial meetings I may be asked to make an assessment of a company's Quality. Over the years I have developed and fine-tuned a set of questions I use to keep the initial assessment as simple and short as possible. Using these questions, I can quickly gain an understanding of a company's concept, belief, awareness, commitment, and understanding of Quality and its contribution to bottom-line results.

My goal is simplicity. The 13 questions below have possible scores ranging from -2 to +3 points; the total possible score is 20 points. This is extremely subjective material and is meant only as a quick guide to assess the existence of a Quality culture. I have used this a number of times with management teams to gain an understanding of their knowledge, awareness, and commitment to Quality. A score of 20 does not necessarily mean that a BBQ culture exists, but it does give an indication as to the company's awareness of and willingness to take the next step to achieve a culture of BBQ. This is just a simple tool that is based upon my experience; it's not scientifically researched or validated, so use it if you like with that disclaimer.

Results of scoring

Less than zero   The company should take affirmative action to increase Quality awareness.

Zero to 10   Quality awareness needs improvement. You likely are not achieving profit potential.

11–14   Quality commitment needs improvement to improve overall company performance.

15–17   Quality commitment likely exists, but positive financial results may not meet full potential.

18–20   A culture of Quality is likely present but will need continuous maintenance to assure sustainability and achievement of profit potential.

1. Can you articulate why Quality matters?

Other than the institutional and expected answers (cost, Quality control, and Quality assurance), if the answer includes anything related to compliance, prevention, and improvement as noted in this book score one point for each reference (possible **Score Zero to 3**).

2. Can you articulate what Quality functions are?

The easiest answers are control/inspection and assurance/auditing, earning zero points. **Score 1** point for the additional mention of any of the following functions: process improvement, business excellence, Lean or Six Sigma, root cause analysis (of failures), failure analysis, reliability.

3. Who owns Quality?

Anything other than "I do" or "my department does" **Score Zero**; otherwise **Score 1** point.

4. Can you identify where Quality belongs in your company?

Subjective question; **Score 1** if the answer mentions nearness to top decision maker.

5. Does your management team understand the difference between Quality control and Quality assurance?

The easiest answer earning a **Score 1** would be inspection (control) and compliance to industry standards (i.e., ISO, ASME, etc.) through auditing (assurance). **Score 1 bonus** point if improvement is added as part of assurance. Although this is not an optimal location for this activity (as noted in this book), it is worth a point for the recognition.

6. Can you describe how to achieve Quality or how to sustain it?

Score -1 if the answer references more inspection or auditing. **Score 1** if the answer articulates any form of strategy related to continuous improvement or prevention. **Score 1 bonus** point if management talks positively about behaviors of Quality. **Score 2 bonus** points if the manager references compliance, prevention, and improvement as parts of BBQ.

7. Does your company have a Quality policy? Where is it?

Score 1 for a "Yes" answer. **Score 1 bonus** point if the person can point you to a public location where the policy is available for employee view.

8. Quality is more than nice words in a vision statement or a policy statement. Do your employees believe in and practice Quality?

Inspection and assurance practices do not qualify as an answer. **Score 1** if the person can either demonstrate or provide an example of how Quality is practiced. Answers must include words such as: prevention, continuous improvement, reduction in defects, and waste reduction (in conjunction with reduction of non-conformances).

9. What do your customers think of your company's Quality?

Score 1 for any answer that indicates that the person is aware of customer's comments and can site a customer name.

10. **Does your company have a strategy for Quality?**

    This is not about Quality policy. **Score 1** if the answer indicates that there is a strategy in place to improve Quality and that it contains a contribution from every department in the company. This is the only acceptable answer. **Score -1** if the answer is "No" or I am not aware of one.

11. **Does your manager's actions reflect behaviors that support your Quality policy?**

    Score Zero if there is no Quality policy; **Score -1** for a "No"; **Score 1** for "Yes" only if there is a Quality policy.

12. **Does the company's top executive demonstrate though actions his/her support of and belief in the Quality policy?**

    Score Zero if there is no Quality policy; **Score -2** for a "No" answer if there is a Quality policy; **Score 1** for "Yes" answer.

13. **Is Quality part of your company culture? Can you provide an example?**

    You may need to define culture: Do people think and behave during their work day as though Quality matters? Do they take accountability for the Quality of their work, and feel free to stop any process that is not exhibiting sound Quality behaviors? Or are they more focused on delivering your company's product or services? For an answer of "No," **Score -1**. **Score 1** if the person can provide an answer demonstrating the above concept of culture.

Glossary

Acronym	Definition
A/P	Accounts payable; usually part of the finance organization
AOP	Annual operating plan; typically, a budget, profit, and growth strategy used in larger companies
ASME	American Society of Mechanical Engineers
ASQ	American Society for Quality; a knowledge-based global community of Quality professionals dedicated to promoting and advancing Quality tools, principles, and practices in their workplaces and communities
BBQ	Behavior Based Quality
BE	Business excellence; typically, a department challenged with improving processes within departments in a company
CEO	Chief executive officer; typically, the top decision maker in a company's hierarchy
COO	Chief operations or operating officer; typically, the person reporting to the CEO who has responsibility and accountability of operational activities of a company

COPQ	Cost of poor Quality; the measure of non-conformances that reflects the dollar impact process and/or product and service errors
CPI	In this book compliance, prevention, and improvement, the three tenets of Behavior Based Quality
CTO	Chief technical officer; usually the top technical strategist reporting to the COO or CEO who has responsibility for the technical advancement of a company's product offerings
DFx	Design for x, where "x" stands for any of the following: manufacturability, repairability, serviceability, reliability, testing, and so forth. The intent of DFx is that a product has been designed with consideration to one or more of the "ilities" noted above
DMAIC	Define, measure, analyze (or assess), improve, control; the basis of Lean manufacturing and process improvement and corrective action
DNA	Deoxyribonucleic acid, a molecule in all living things that carries the genetic code for reproduction and growth
DPMO	Defects per million opportunities, used to calculate the "Sigma" level of Quality. 6 Sigma level of Quality indicates that a process generates 3.4 defects for 1 million possible occurrences of defects in the process.
FPY	First-pass yield, a measure of testing and inspection; the number of failures or rejects as a percent of the total inspected or tested
G&A	General and administrative (costs), an accounting/budget term describing general nonmanufacturing administrative costs

HR	Human resources, the department responsible for establishing policy related to the hiring and management of employees
HSE	Health, safety and environment, typically the department responsible for overseeing safety policies and culture
ISO	International Organization for Standardization, a membership organization bringing together experts to share knowledge and develop voluntary, consensus-based, market-relevant international standards
KPI	Key performance indicators, specific metrics (often financial) used to track company performance
MRP	Material requirements planning, the process of setting up the purchase, stocking, and distribution to manufacturing or service functions of parts, accessories, and consumables
MTBF	Mean time between failures
MTTF	Mean time to failure
MTTR	Mean time to repair
NDT	Nondestructive testing (nondestructive inspection), the process of testing or inspecting product without bringing damage or harm to the end product (e.g., X-ray examination)
OTD	On-time delivery, often used as a measure of delivery performance
P&L	Profit and loss, the term used to describe actions related to budgeting, planning, and reporting on planned or actual conditions from a financial perspective
Q1	Quarter, as in first quarter of a year

QA	Quality assurance; typically the department assigned to assure compliance to industry standards (e.g., ISO) and internal processes
QC	Quality control; typically the department assigned to perform inspections upon receipt of material and throughout the manufacturing process
QMS	Quality management system; a formalized system that documents processes, procedures, and responsibilities for achieving Quality policies and objectives
R&D	Research and development, the department or function responsible for researching and developing new technologies and the integration of those technologies into company products
RCA	Root cause analysis
RFQ	Request for quote
RIF	Reduction in force, the process of reducing headcount (layoffs)
ROI	Return on investment, the amount of dollars an investment returns compared to the cost of the investment
SBC	Safety based culture; the HSE approach to BBQ
SDP	Strategic deployment process; one of the tools used to define and implement a financial plan for a company's five-year growth with specific focus on year one
SIPOC	Supplier, input, process, output, customer; the cornerstone tool used in process development in Lean manufacturing. Defining requirements for each of these elements is integral to building defect-free processes. Understanding and using this approach is an essential behavior in BBQ.

SMART
(as in Metrics)
Specific (strategic), measurable, accurate (attainable or achievable), reliable (realistic or relevant), and timely

SME
Subject matter expert

SQDC
Safety, Quality, delivery, cost; the philosophy defined in the "Toyota Way." If you put safety and Quality first, delivery and cost (improvement or profit) will naturally follow. When you put delivery or cost in front of safety or Quality, both will suffer.

TPO
Third-party operator, typically a consultant or contractor used in addition to company employees

TRIR
Total recordable incident rate; the OSHA (Occupational Safety and Health Administration) metric imposed on companies by the U.S. federal government to report safety incidents as related to number of man hours worked in a given time period

TTI
Target to improve; used in the SDP process to define a key metric in a format of Improve X from Y to Z by date. Done properly this is a SMART metric.

TTM
Time to market, the measure of a product concept from inception through design and manufacturing to first release to the intended market

TTP
Time to profitability; a measure of how long it takes a product to achieve profitability from its point of release to the market (similar to ROI)

VP
Vice president

Index

Note: page numbers in *italics* indicate figures and tables.

W-Y

Z

About the Author

With a background in industries ranging from high-tech commercial and consumer electronics and network communications equipment to light and heavy manufacturing in the energy sector, Mr. Angle has built a broad spectrum of experience in mid-level to executive roles ranging from operations, supply chain, Quality, engineering, and project management.

This background has allowed him to develop critical thinking skills needed to understand an organization's strengths and weaknesses, identify external threats and opportunities, and define and adopt strategies for changing conditions while developing initiatives to achieve organizational goals and objectives. He coaches and mentors cross-functional teams to achieve exceptional rather than expected results that look beyond the quick, often not sustainable tactical fix to prevention-based strategic initiatives that achieve long-term sustainable results. His educational background includes a bachelor's degree in industrial technologies with a master's degree in systems management. The combination provides a unique perspective of the integration of supporting system processes that bring about profitable results.

Mr. Angle attributes his success to his passion for positive change and collaboration with decision makers to develop workable solutions and implementation plans while providing effective communication and building consensus and commitment to change. During the process or change, he prepares and supports those affected by change by monitoring transitions, providing counsel, and evaluating results.

www.ingramcontent.com/pod-product-compliance
Lightning Source LLC
Chambersburg PA
CBHW052111230326
41599CB00055B/5676